The Life and Death of King Edward

Joshua Gray

Forever Press
2017

Published by

Forever Press
PO Box 263
Somerville MA 02143

Copyright ©2017

ISBN 978-0-9989289-0-6

All images used in this book are courtesy
of Wikimedia Commons or derived
from pre-1930 print sources.

The cover image is the Welbeck portrait
of the Earl of Oxford, Paris, circa 1575,
courtesy of Wikimedia Commons.

Printed in the USA
By CS/Amazon

For Dad

"There is no greater agony than bearing an untold story inside you." – Maya Angelou,
I Know Why the Caged Bird Sings

"And in fact [Shakespeare's] works are so much more glorious than any actual reign could have been. When we think of the age of Elizabeth, we think first of all of Shakespeare. So, he has grasped that kingship, but in his own way."
– Charles Beauclerk

Table of Contents

Foreword	i
Introduction	vi
How to read this book	xii
Dramatis Personae	xiii

INDUCTIONS (1548, 1590s-1600s, 1623)

Background notes	1
Dear Diary	3
The Clown	4
The Joker	6

ACT I (1560s)

Background Notes	8
Dear Lord Burghley	10
Please Tell me	11
My Dear Sister	12
My Earliest Teacher	14
Caius and the Fowle	15
An Astonishing Man	16
Letter in Fluent French to William Cecil	18

ACT II (1569-1576)

Background Notes	20
I see a Bastard	24

Weeks Later	25
My Own Daughter	26
Bed Trick	27
My Dearest Anne	28
Frobisher's Expedition of 1576	29
Shake-speare's Renaissance	30
Spendthrift Tymon	31
You *Must* Be a Bastard	32
The Biggest Query of My Life	33

ACT III (1574-1586)
Background notes	35
A One-sided Conversation in Bath	38
Seven Italian Towns and Memories Thereof	40
The Catholic among Protestants	42
Spain Threatens	43
The Fool is a Truth Teller	44
The First Henry Tetralogy	45
Reunited with Anne	46

ACT IV (1587-1603)
Background notes	47
A Letter to Horace	50
You Wrong Me	51
Code Words	52
Much Ado about the Bastard	53
Wide Awake Afterwards	54
The Bastard	55
Elizabeth Thinks as She Paces	56
Edgar/Edward/Edmund	58

Essex Rebellion	59
Surreal	60

ACT V (1590-1603)
Background Notes	61
Sonnets: Dedication and Prologue	63
Sonnets: First 26	64
Sonnets: First 50 of 100	70
Sonnets: Second 50 of 100	81
Sonnets: Second 26	93
Sonnets: Epilogue	99

EPITAPH (1601-1603)
Background notes	101
Phoenix and Turtle - Threnos	103
Bibliography/Suggested Reading	105
About the Author	111

The Life and Death of King Edward

Foreword

For most readers Shakespeare's sonnets are an indecipherable mess—and that includes boatloads of Shakespeare scholars, who tend to dismiss the sonnets as "a poetic exercise," where we see "the young writer sharpening his craft" and so on. So, for most of us, it's okay just to enjoy the half-dozen poems most literate people are familiar with and forget about the rest. It may nag at them that they haven't read, let alone understood, all the sonnets, but then again, how many of us have? Without some clue, some roadmap into what they are about, they can easily seem to be dense, repetitive, organized in no particular way, and fairly uninteresting … even though the poet was obviously writing about something extremely important to him.

The few mainstream expert scholarly commentaries that are available are equally hopeless in getting at what story lies behind the sonnets. They speculate about the shadowy characters that seem to populate the poems—a mysterious dark lady? A young nobleman with whom the Stratford glover's son had a homosexual relationship? Were there two young men? Was there a rival poet, and, if so, who was he? In short, the "expert" commentaries are as confusing as the poems.

But in recent years that has changed, thanks to the Shakespeare authorship debate, and to the efforts of the Oxfordian movement (those who believe that Edward de Vere, 17th

Earl of Oxford was the true Shakespeare), which has helped to change the Shakespeare studies landscape over the past thirty years and to push it more towards trying to understand the works of Shakespeare through understanding the life that Shakespeare lived. As this book goes to press in 2017 there are books, stage plays, movies and television shows coming out trying to flesh out the life of the man from Stratford (whose real name, by the way—at his birth and in his will—was "Shaksper," not the London pen-name "Shake-speare") and make some sense of how and why he wrote his plays and poems. All these recent mainstream efforts to make Shakespeare real are happening because of the pressure from the Oxfordian movement. But all such efforts still come up short, since, with the wrong author in mind, there is in fact no way to ever get at the right story behind the sonnets.

Even Oxfordians themselves have had trouble getting at the story behind the sonnets, and have argued over the true story for decades. A major break-through occurred in the late 1990s, when Oxfordian scholar Hank Whittemore began publishing his findings on the hidden story the sonnets were telling (eventually published in 2005, *The Monument*). From this new perspective we have since come to know more or less exactly what the Poet of the Sonnets (i.e., Oxford) intended them to be, namely a carefully constructed literary monument to his son by Queen Elizabeth, an unacknowledged love-child named Henry Wriothesley, 3rd Earl of Southampton.

The Life and Death of King Edward

The sonnets are a record of Oxford's attempt to persuade the queen to (1) drop the whole Virgin Queen myth; (2) acknowledge their son as the legitimate heir to the throne, thereby carrying on the Tudor line (known in Oxfordian circles as the "Prince Tudor" theory); (3) forgive Southampton for his part in the Essex Rebellion and not chop off his head. Many sonnets are directed to Southampton, and tell the story of the terrible price Oxford had to pay to save his life. It's an amazing story, and for those really interested in the subject, we recommend Hank Whittemore's magnum opus *The Monument* and Peter Rush's *Hidden In Plain Sight*, both of which detail how meticulously organized the 154 sonnets are, and how each fits into the timeline of Southampton's life (see the Bibliography/Suggested Reading for a selected list of books on the sonnets and on the Oxfordian perspective on them).

Over the past 15 years this new perspective on the sonnets has spread and new books have fleshed out and expanded on what Whittemore's *The Monument* first put in place.

This present volume came to be when one of those influenced by *The Monument*, poet Joshua Gray, reduced every one of the sonnets to poetic tweets—14 lines of dense, complicated verse condensed to 140 characters organized in easy-to-understand quatrains that stand on their own as excellent poems.

Gray's quatrains shed light on how the sonnets can be seen as chapters in a story. In his perceptive translations (if that is the right word) he strips away the camouflage Oxford had to employ to keep his identity a secret. The poet's complicated and always difficult relationship with his sovereign and his son is unmasked, while the astonishing story the sonnets relate finally becomes clear.

In *The Life and Death of King Edward*, these original "sonnet tweets" have been given a "prequel" by a series of poems (Acts I-IV) that delve deeper into the hidden story behind their author, Edward de Vere, 17th Earl of Oxford, and how and why he chose to become "Shake-speare" in the 1590s.

This deeper hidden story is based on the basic Oxfordian theory of Shakespeare (i.e., that "Shake-speare" was really a pseudonym for Edward de Vere) *and* the theory that de Vere was not just the father of a son by Queen Elizabeth (the original "Prince Tudor" theory, dating back to the 1930s), but that he was also himself a son of Queen Elizabeth, born in 1548 when the teenage princess was rumored to have been seduced (and perhaps impregnated) by Thomas Seymour. This more recent theory (called within the Oxfordian movement the "Prince Tudor II" theory) was part of Roland Emmerich's 2011 Shakespeare authorship film *Anonymous*. It is, to put it mildly, controversial.

At that time Oxfordians' greatest concern about this film was that, by focusing on these sexual escapades of the Virgin Queen and Shakespeare (i.e., not just adultery, but also incest), both the Oxfordian movement and the Shakespeare authorship debate itself would come under attack for a theory that many Oxfordians do not accept, and further, one which actually appalls them. And yet it is a theory that helps make sense of many of the Shakespeare plays and poems (especially the poems), of the strange history at the end of the Tudor dynasty (why couldn't Elizabeth have simply named a successor, as nearly all monarchs in history do, as their duty to the nation?), and — finally, but most importantly — of the infamous Essex Rebellion of 1601 (why was Southampton spared execution, and how could Shakespeare not have been punished at all for his play *Richard II* which seemingly supported the rebellion?).

We invite readers to experience this whole, bizarre story through Gray's poems, and put their own perspectives on Shakespeare's life and history, and of the very notion of "authorship," to the test.

William Boyle
June 2017

Introduction

When I was fourteen years old, my dad, Patrick Prentice, took me to his parents' second home in the mountains. While the week was eventful, the most interesting part of it was watching my father on the ground floor reading a fat book. It was Charlton Ogburn's *The Mysterious William Shakespeare*, and it transformed my father into an Oxfordian, that is, a person who believes Edward de Vere, the 17th Earl of Oxford, was the true author of the works of Shakespeare. Wanting to be like my dad, I also called myself an Oxfordian.

But it wasn't until high school and college that I read Shakespeare. My college Shakespeare class bored me to tears. I decided I hated Shakespeare. I really couldn't understand why his characters never communicated with each other. Why didn't Othello just ask Desdemona if she did anything with the handkerchief? I called my dad from the dorm's phone booth after receiving my poor grade and complained. Interestingly, he had an excellent answer for why Othello didn't just ask Desdemona, but the answer was only really good if one stops believing the status quo. Truth was really important to Edward de Vere because his life was full of lies and untruths. If no one told him the truth in real life, then as a lived experience he put it in the plays as well. Even if Desdemona is asked, her truth would not be believed by Othello. And in some plays like *Hamlet*, characters have no reason to ask the truth, but the audience is the jury for what the truth is. For Oxford, Truth is the metaphor that shows up in all the Shakespeare plays and sonnets.

That's right: the answer was in the authorship question, the question of who really wrote the works. Oxford. I was hooked. For the next twenty years I listened to my dad's arguments. I've wanted to write about the theory for fifteen years, and started several outlines, but I had no idea how to structure it (I also didn't know enough).

Eventually, Cameron Conaway's *Until You Make the Shore* and Frank X. Walker's *Isaac Murphy: I Dedicate This Ride* provided that structure. During the summer of 2010, as I was recovering from surgery after a melanoma diagnosis (see my book *Symposium*), my dad was in England as a consultant to the film *Anonymous*, and just a few months later he was a producer of a documentary on the topic, along with two other producers (Lisa and Laura Wilson), called *Last Will. and Testament.* But even at that point, I had done no research on my own.

In 2014 I told Dad I wanted to really understand the Oxfordian argument, and his documentary was what did it. I read just about everything I could. Most of these books used Oxford's biography as evidence, and so, finally, the plays began to make complete sense to me. But it was the sonnets---the elusive sonnets---that still remained the collective elephant in the room. Reading Hank Whittemore's *The Monument* changed that. *The Monument* takes the entire sequence and breaks it down sonnet by sonnet, line by line, word by word. It single handedly brought the sonnets into the conversation. And the more I read about Oxford as the author, and the enormous evidence supporting him, the more I understood it was him.

Many traditional scholars (those who believe the man from Stratford is the author) believe the sonnets are a neat exercise; they believe this because they cannot otherwise explain their existence. But every writer knows that you don't do something so large and significant merely as an exercise. My problem was that I never could understand them. Even as I read *The Monument*, I began to realize that just reading it, sonnet by sonnet, still wasn't going to be effective for me. So for mere understanding's sake, as I read each sonnet and Whittemore's explanation, I also reduced each one to a quatrain. I essentially took all the fluff out, and took them to the bare bones. Then I tweeted them, every one of them. Reducing them this way finally allowed me to understand them for the first time. And the bonus of reading and understanding the sonnets is that it explains the true story of Edward de Vere's scandalous life, a life that included his close relationship with Queen Elizabeth.

Elizabeth I became known as the Virgin Queen, because she was famously married to her people instead of one man. It was a political success, and the people knew she had their best interest in mind. But privately, she almost certainly had a love life and a sex life. As a teenager of sixteen she was either raped or seduced by her "uncle" (by marriage) Thomas Seymour, and if his destiny (he was executed a year later in 1549) has anything to say about it, it was probably rape. There were rumors at the time of a pregnancy and of a possible child, but nothing was certain. Over the years some Oxfordians have come to believe that Edward de Vere was that child, later secretly placed in the household of the 16th Earl of Oxford, and after his death, becoming a royal ward---a child of the court.

This theory of Oxford as Elizabeth's child is one part of what is known in Oxfordian circles as the Prince Tudor theory. After the 16th Earl died, Edward, age fourteen, was brought to the heart of court, and lived with William Cecil (Elizabeth's Lord Treasurer), who was, effectively, his new father. As he was a royal ward of the court, Elizabeth was in effect his official "mother." After age twenty-one he was in the highest favor with Elizabeth and the two of them were rumored to be close. This is where the rest of the Prince Tudor theory enters the picture, for some Oxfordians have theorized that their relationship was indeed very close, and that it resulted in the birth of a boy who was placed in the household of the 2nd Earl of Southampton. This boy was Henry Wriothesley, the 3rd Earl of Southampton, the famous Fair Youth of the sonnets. And if both halves of the Prince Tudor theory are true (i.e., that Oxford is both a son of the Queen and later the father of a child by her), then this is incest.

Incest: a lot of people cringe at that word — "There's no way that can happen!" But incest was how some monarchies throughout history have produced their blood heirs. It certainly is taboo, but it has happened. I once worked with teenage daughters who were the victims of fatherly incest; but mother-son incest is, to most people, the most shocking of all, since the mother is the "nurturer" of the child, the one who suckles it. Therefore such a relationship is seen as the most unacceptable of all, a betrayal.

But what about the case of estranged mothers and sons, a relationship that involves no nurturing or suckling? For if Elizabeth was in fact Edward de Vere's biological mother, she clearly had not been the one who raised him---she was not his nurturer. It might surprise you, but we have a modern version of such a relationship involving a modern celebrity that might be instructive in considering what may have happened in Elizabeth's England centuries ago.

The 2010 movie *Nowhere Boy* depicts the teenage years of John Lennon, who was raised by his Aunt Mimi, his mother Julia's sister. His mother had left him when he was about five and only came back into his life when he was in his teens. She was beautiful, he was a teenager, and they fell in love. His friends and other members of the Quarrymen (Lennon's first musical group) were aware of both their parent-child relationship, and yet also how they seemed to be almost like a couple "dating"; no one knows how intimate they actually became, but some wondered.

Lennon had been raised by his strict, tightly-wound aunt, while his biological mother was, in effect, a free-spirited stranger.

The Life and Death of King Edward

When they reconnected, she was the one who introduced him to music, and bought him his first guitar, which eventually led him to fame and fortune. Of course it wasn't Julia's free spirit that made him fall in love with her. She was his mother, after all, but he didn't *know* her as a mother. He knew her simply as a new girl in the neighborhood.

    I chose to write this story as poetry because I'm a poet. I've been asked why I didn't write it in Shakespeare's language. The answer is that I thought about it, but decided to write in modern English because my main goal is to provide understanding to my readers. It also offered a chance to create dramatic scenes with dialogue, revealing the "character" of my characters. Elizabeth has a potty mouth; William Cecil is aloof; Edward, the author of plays full of profanity and insults, is a courtier who doesn't use profanity himself. I can't do these sorts of things in Shakespearean language.
    But the main reason I used poetry is for the sake of anyone who hates lengthy documentaries and nonfiction (and I know quite a few). There are already many scholarly, nonfiction Oxfordian books out there. I needed a way to reach other audiences. There needed to be another way to tell the story.

Joshua Gray
March 5, 2017
Berea, KY

Joshua Gray

HOW TO READ THIS BOOK

The book is presented in the format of a play — a total of seven sections that include an Induction, five Acts, and an Epitaph. All these sections are presented in chronological order, beginning in 1548 and ending in 1603. Each section includes a note indicating its time period.

All sections also begin with "Background Notes" (some basic historical facts that pertain to the time period and the poems in that section), followed by some key excerpts from some of the Shakespeare plays and/or other documents that show how Oxford himself was always commenting on his life in his plays and poems. I strongly urge readers to read these notes in order to fully understand the poems in each act.

When reading the poems please note:

- Within poems, brackets ([]) specify a Shakespearean aside.
- Italics justified right are dialogue from the other character in the poem.
- All other italics are for emphasis
- The sonnets (Act V) are different. They are broken into sections and chapters as found in Hank Whittemore's *The Monument* (2005). Each section is introduced with a compressed version of Whittemore's original commentary.
- With few colloquial exceptions, there are no contractions within Acts I-IV.

The Life and Death of King Edward

Dramatis Personae

SHAKSPER, a clown

EDWARD, "Eddie" de Vere, 17th Earl of Oxford and Lord Great Chamberlain of England. A poet on the grandest scale.

EARL JOHN, Edward's father

WILLIAM "Undad" Cecil, Guardian of the State, chief minister to Elizabeth

HORACE "Horatio" Vere, Edward's cousin

HENRY Wriothesley, Edward's bastard son by Queen Elizabeth

ROBERT Cecil, William's son and future Chief Minister

MARGERY (Golding) Vere, Edward's mother

MARY Vere, Edward's sister

ELIZABETH Vere, Edward's daughter

KATHERINE, Edward's half-sister

ANNE Cecil, William's daughter and Edward's first wife

ELIZABETH "Liz" Tudor, Queen of England

Teacher, students, boy

Scene: London and its environs

Joshua Gray

The Life and Death of King Edward

INDUCTIONS
(1548, 1590s-1600s, 1623)

Background Notes

Ten years before the Elizabethan Age began in 1558 with the coronation of Queen Elizabeth the young princess Elizabeth had an infamous encounter with her "uncle"/guardian Lord Admiral Thomas Seymour in 1548. Some say she was impregnated at that time and that a child may have been born. Elizabeth denied it.

Decades later, in a small town northeast of London, the young son of a wool merchant may have attended school. That he existed is certain. That he was educated at all is unproven. That he was highly educated in a grammar school is virtually impossible. When this young son grew up all existing contemporaneous records identify him as a businessman, not a writer.

Many decades later, in 1623, the greatest writer in Western letters, "William Shakespeare," is preserved for eternity in a printed Folio. All of his plays were included in it, but none of his poems. The image on the cover is not life-like, but is all we have. Who was he?

Joshua Gray

Related plays and poems: The Rape of Lucrece, Venus and Adonis, Troilus and Cressida

"I am 'sort of' haunted by the conviction that the divine William is the biggest and most successful fraud ever practiced on a patient world." -- Henry James (1843-1916)

"When Shakespeare died in Stratford IT WAS NOT AN EVENT...Nobody came down from London; there were no lamenting poems, no eulogies, no national tears--there was merely silence, and nothing more...No praiseful voice was lifted for the lost Bard of Avon; even Ben Jonson waited seven years before he lifted his." -- Mark Twain, *Is Shakespeare Dead?* (1909)

"The man from Stratford seems to have nothing at all to justify his claim, whereas Oxford has everything."-- Sigmund Freud, *Autobiographical Study*, 1927

"Leave Stratford, go to London, go to Court. That's where your answer is." -- William Boyle, in *Last Will. & Testament* (2011)

"Be Daly Prove you shall me fynde
To be to you bothe loving and kynde."
 -- Anne Boleyn, in a note to Henry VIII

In the 1500s, "loving" and "kynde" both had double meanings: spouse and child, respectively. It seems Anne believed she was both his wife and daughter. Consider a more precise reading in Hamlet's opening line, after his uncle addresses him (*Hamlet*, I.ii.66):

> [Aside] A little more than kin, and less than kind.

"Happy" is also a word with a double meaning: royal. And when one is twice royal, as Boleyn thought, one is most happy.

The Life and Death of King Edward

DEAR DIARY
Princess Elizabeth

My fucking father, my mother
died fucking a monster. So many lives
lost for a boy. Today,

I bore a son. I am married to no man.
God damn sons. Fucking rape. Flirting
doesn't mean...Christ!

What is Seymour? No more
a kind uncle. My honor, violated.
Who am I?

I told William to take the boy away;
do not kill him. He is mine --
but no man, no boy claims me.

And I will not chase for love.
Neither man, nor boar. No, mother,
I will not be *most happy*.

Figure 1 - Princess Elizabeth in the Tower

Joshua Gray

THE CLOWN

Enter Shaksper and a teacher from one end, secondary students from another.

TEACHER: Class, today I brought a special guest. He is a popular poet and playwright, and has a current production at The Globe. Please welcome, William Shakespeare!

Enter a boy, who stays downstage, listening.

SHAKSPER: Hello!

STUDENT 1: You're not a writer! You can't read or write!

SHAKSPER: Why do you say that?

STUDENT 1: Because I've seen your signature. It's appalling!

STUDENT 2: Is that true? You didn't go to the grade school?

SHAKSPER: As a matter of fact, I did.

STUDENT 2: Prove it! Can't, can you. Because the school burned down years ago!

SHAKSPER: Still coulda gone! Anyway doctors have bad signatures. Doesn't mean I'm illiterate.

BOY: *(walking over)* But you are, cuz I am too.

The Life and Death of King Edward

STUDENT 2: Who are you?

BOY: I'm his son.

SHAKSPER: I don't know that kid. Look, I never left England. But there's proof I'm the author.

TEACHER: Proof? Where? The playwright wrote mostly about Italy, including detailed descriptions about Italian landscapes.

BOY: Dad, where are your copies of the plays? Not in our house. Anyway, you're a businessman.

TEACHER: A businessman? I thought I recognized you. Make-up can't hide your eyes. You took my husband to small claims court. And you charged me for the wine you served me when we were discussing this class visit!

(Shaksper is chased offstage. Exeunt.)

Figure 2 - From Minerva Britanna: "Lo here deceite doth stand"

Joshua Gray

THE JOKER

"Have you ever studied that picture, that face? It's totally unreal." --Sir Derek Jacobi

"But since he cannot, reader, looke
Not on his picture, but his booke."-- Ben Jonson

The joker has two right eyes. A line
divides chinny chin chin
and earlobe: a mask.

His head suspends above
shoulders, the right arm
merely a clone of the left.

Renaissance art entertains
amazing perspective.
Perspective is not a problem
so much as an expensive image of a joke.

Figure 3 - The First Folio

Joshua Gray

ACT I

(1550s to 1560s)

Background Notes

Edward de Vere, 17th Earl of Oxford (1550-1604), is a child prodigy whose father, John de Vere, suddenly died at age 46, when Edward was twelve.

Fourteen years earlier (1548) John de Vere had married Margery Golding (sister of the writer and scholar Arthur Golding), after a very strange turn of events. He was bound in June 1548 to marry one Dorothy Fosser (who would have been his second wife) when suddenly — through the intervention of Edward Seymour, Lord Protector of the boy King Edward VI and brother of Lord Admiral Thomas Seymour — he instead married Margery Golding (August 1, 1548). Clearly something unusual had happened, but what was it? And why?

After his father's death in 1562 Oxford inherited, among other things, a troupe of players. He completed his childhood and his schooling as a royal ward, living in the household of Queen Elizabeth's chief counselor, William Cecil (later Lord Burghley), a strict man. His mother Margery and his sister Mary did not live with him.

Oxford is a remarkable young man, even unique. His teachers all say so. He undergoes (and thrives under) a strict academic regime, with his uncle Arthur Golding one of several tutors. But he also chaffs under the strict control of his surrogate father, William Cecil. His 1563 letter to Cecil (written in French) reveals much of this.

The Life and Death of King Edward

Related Plays: Hamlet, Merchant of Venice, Troilus and Cressida

"I confess that a large trust hath been committed to me, of those things which in my Lord's lifetime was kept most secret from me." — Margery Vere (Edward's mother) in a 1560s letter to Cecil

> Earl John was a generous patron of theatrical arts, and sponsored a theater troupe that included some of the best actors in the country. During winter the troupe stayed at Hedingham Castle, and the troupe's fool (possibly the unemployed jester from Henry VIII's court) could have easily attracted Edward as a child. In 1562, Earl John was only in his mid-forties when he died. There were no signs of failing health, yet he changed his will a month before to Edward's benefit, and he made an abrupt and failed attempt at an arranged marriage for the boy. Some historians suspect murder, perhaps by Cecil himself.

"To write a history of England between 1548 and 1590 is to tell the story of Cecil." — John Culverhouse, Curator, Burghley House

HORATIO: My lord, I think I saw him yesternight.
HAMLET: Saw? Who?
HORATIO: My lord, the king your father.
HAMLET: The king my father! — *Hamlet*, I.11.196.

> Horace was de Vere's favorite cousin and was also called Horatio.

"In *Hamlet* Shakespeare has revealed too much of himself." — Frank Harris, *The Man Shakespeare and His Tragic Life Story* (1911)

William Cecil's and Polonius' precepts are eerily alike.

YOUNG LUCIUS: Grandsire, 'tis Ovid's *Metamorphoses*; My mother gave it me. *Titus Andronicus*, IV.1.42.

Joshua Gray

DEAR LORD BURGHLEY
Margery

I write again to ask
about Earl John's estate.

For Hedingham is home.
Only two women live here:
a recent widow, and a too young, too soon.

You know for years Earl John
kept a large secret from me. (Edward.)
I will be silent.

And so, please?

What of his estate?

Figure 4. - Castle Hedingham

The Life and Death of King Edward

PLEASE TELL ME
Mary

Father adored you.
I still remember his face:

his eyes were stars,
his smile warm,
his laugh loud and jolly.
A man who loved life.

Please tell me

how you are,
why you are so long
where you are.

Mother doesn't speak.

Joshua Gray

MY DEAR SISTER
Edward

Our indifferent mother doesn't speak
because of who she interred.
I still grieve, and see Father, in dreams.

Summers, we talked and walked
around the wall, or went to the moat.
The mosquitoes were monstrous.

A daily routine, if he wasn't at Court
and I at school.

Soon before he died, on one of these walks,
he told me about his crude philosophy
on the female sex. I did not understand why,

but now I believe he
knew he would die. Was he telling me
not to be like him? But finally

I understood his mistreatment of Mother
was chronic. A kind, gentle, jolly man.
And a loose cannon.

Winters, his troupe stayed at Hedingham,
their lodge our dungeon.
How we snuck in and just listened!

Now, I have a new father. A boorish,
narrow-minded, puritanical *auf.*
Dinner, he preaches precepts, till we vomit.

He is Lord Burghley, the Queen's Spirit,
aid, and advisor. I am a child of the State,
and will grow up here. An unfortunate fate.

O horrible, horrible, most horrible!

Figure 5 - William Cecil, made Lord Burghley in 1571 by Queen Elizabeth.

Joshua Gray

MY EARLIEST TEACHER
Edward

Sir Thomas Smith, at Ankerwicke.

I remember a picture
in a table, that hanging
of cosmology, and three curiously
painted pictures.

So many books of all kinds
to learn from: Latin, French, Greek,
Italian, Spanish, Hebrew.
So many Classical authors.
Such detailed law.
Hawking and Hunting.

I was a decade old
when I enrolled in his college.

The Life and Death of King Edward

CAIUS AND THE FOWLE
Edward

Professor John Caius is a man of medicine.
A catholic like me. A great advisor.
I am happy
Liz named him to her Court.

Ever notice that Caius is the name
of the French doctor in *Merry Wives*
and Earl of Kent's nom de plume in *Lear*?

Thomas Fowle, you say?
I don't remember him.
I don't remember a damn thing.

Joshua Gray

AN ASTONISHING MAN
Edward

1.

I do not love living
with William, but
I love the library.
So many books,
so much to learn.

Outside the library,
too many European
scholars and politicians.
I cannot handle them all.
I hear his enemies
call him King Cecil.

I know why.
He controls me,
or tries to. Ed:
be more proper
don't read that, read this
you can't go out
stay away from the pub.

The Life and Death of King Edward

2.

What are you reading, Ed?

Words, words, words.

How do you find it?

Your books are well catalogued.

I mean, how is the book.

It says old men lack wit. And want to be crabs.

Crabs?

To go backward. In time. Be young.

You're crazy. You need to go outside.

Into my grave?

That is indeed outside.

Joshua Gray

LETTER IN FLUENT FRENCH TO WILLIAM CECIL, TRANSLATED
Edward

Most kind and honorable Sir,

Leave.
    Me.
        Alone.

I most appreciate your last hire,
he taught well, though briefly.
His copy of *Beowulf*, the only one
in existence, unpublished,
I might use it to tell our story.

But he quit his post.
And I am thirteen.

I now have a teacher *I* selected.
He wrote the most beautiful translation
of Ovid's *Metamorphoses* I've read so far.

He is also my uncle and lawyer.
Yes, Arthur Golding is my instructor.

I appreciate your concern for my well-being.
I now control it.

Figure 6 – 1563 letter in French to William Cecil

Joshua Gray

ACT II

(1569 – 1576)

Background Notes

Oxford in 1569 changes his signature into an elaborate crown-like image, which seems to be symbolizing "something." He uses this new signature throughout his life, right up until the death of Queen Elizabeth in 1603. Then he abruptly stops using it.

He is called a bastard more than once by his half-sister Katherine, and even (once) by the Queen.

He is forced to marry William Cecil's teenage daughter Anne in 1571. Cecil is made Lord Burghley at this time in order to facilitate the marriage of a commoner into the nobility.

In January 1575, just before leaving for Italy, Oxford tells Queen Elizabeth that if his wife gives birth, the child is not his. They have had no children after three years of marriage. His wife gives birth to a daughter, Elizabeth, in July 1575. Oxford rejects the child as his, and rejects his wife under suspicion of adultery. She is deeply hurt.

He travels to Italy in 1575-1576 and comes back a changed man. In 1576 his returning ship is attacked by pirates in the English Channel, and he is stripped of his clothes. During his continental travels he had spent everything he had, and wrote to Lord Burghley while traveling for more money, to be raised by selling his estates.

In 1576 he invests £3,000 in Martin Frobisher's first voyage in search of a "Northwest Passage" trade route to China and India. He loses all of it.

The Life and Death of King Edward

Related plays: All's Well That Ends Well, Measure for Measure, Hamlet, The Merchant of Venice, Henry IV Part 2, Timon of Athens, Troilus and Cressida

HAMLET: Do you think I meant country matters?
OPHELIA: I think nothing, my lord.
HAMLET: That's a fair thought to lie between maids' legs.
OPHELIA: What is, my lord?
HAMLET: Nothing. — *Hamlet*, i.iii.

CORDELIA: Nothing, my lord.
KING LEAR: Nothing!
CORDELIA: Nothing.
KING LEAR: Nothing will come of nothing: speak again.

> In the 1500s the word 'nothing' meant what it means today, but was also slang for the woman's sexual organ (men have things, women no-things). Consider that meaning for a more precise interpretation of the above lines. Think also of *Much Ado About Nothing*.

CORDELIA: Good my lord,
You have begot me, bred me, *loved* me: I
Return those duties back as are right fit,
Obey you, love you, and most honour you.
Why have my sisters husbands, if they say
They love you all? Haply, when I shall wed,
That lord whose hand must take my plight shall carry
Half my love with him, half my care and duty:
Sure, I shall never marry like my sisters,
To *love* my father all. — *King Lear*, I.i.92ff.

> [Emphasis mine.] Remember Anne Boleyn's quote ("Be Daly Prove you shall me fynde / To be to you bothe loving and kynde.")? Cordelia is more than Lear's daughter! This is why Lear got so angry. Cordelia's answer is unintentionally ripe with double meaning.

SHYLOCK: Three thousand ducats; well.
BASSANIO: Ay, sir, for three months.
SHYLOCK: For three months; well.

BASSANIO: For the which, as I told you, Antonio shall be bound.
SHYLOCK: Antonio shall become bound; well. —
The Merchant of Venice, I.i.1.

> Meanwhile, Antonio has three ships out to sea that when returned would make him rich. Antonio believes they sank.

"I am but mad North-northwest." *Hamlet* (II.2)

Hamlet was attacked by pirates and stripped of his clothes [*Hamlet* (IV.6)] just as Oxford was in 1576.

Timon is a lost classical play about a philanthropist who became a misanthrope because he spent all his money. Plutarch parenthetically discusses it, while Lucian tells it more fully. Lucian's story was never translated into English, only Latin, French, and Italian.

MISTRESS QUICKLY: A hundred mark is a long one for a poor lone woman to bear: and I have borne, and borne, and borne, and have been fubbed off, and fubbed off, and fubbed off, from this day to that day, that it is a shame to be thought on. —
Henry IV, pt. 2: II.i.

> Quickly has called for Falstaff's arrest for this large debt he owes her.

BERTRAM: Undone, and forfeited to cares for ever!
PAROLLES: What's the matter, sweet-heart?
BERTRAM: Although before the solemn priest I have sworn,
I will not bed her.
PAROLLES: What, what, sweet-heart?
BERTRAM: O my Parolles, they have married me! I'll to the Tuscan wars, and never bed her.
— *All's Well That Ends Well*, II.iii.278ff.

> 'Her' is Helena, who lives in the same house as Bertram. In an earlier scene, his mother wants Helena to call her Mother, and indicates Helena has stayed in the house for a long time. Bertram is essentially asked to marry his sister. He refuses, yet

The Life and Death of King Edward

in the end is "tricked" by Helena into bedding her, though he doesn't know it is her: a bed-trick.

> A bed trick is a set-up. A woman with whom a man doesn't want to sleep arranges an encounter in which the man thinks he's sleeping with a different woman, but in reality he is sleeping with the woman he doesn't want. This unlikely plot device appears in four of Shakespeare's plays (*All's Well that Ends Well, Measure for Measure, Cymbeline,* and *The Two Noble Kinsman*). It is also mentioned in A *History and Topography of the County of Essex* (1831) as something which actually happened to Edward de Vere by his wife Anne, as a result of a "stratagem" of his father-in-law, William Cecil.

In *Hamlet*, Ophelia is Polonius' daughter. Polonius is the Queen's chief advisor, and has been for a long time. Ophelia then feels like a sister to Hamlet. In the Court of Queen Elizabeth William Cecil (upon whom, most scholars agree, Polonius is modeled) is the monarch's chief advisor. He has a daughter, Anne (i.e., Ophelia), who is married to Edward de Vere (i.e., Hamlet). They grew up together in William Cecil's household in the 1560s. Oxfordian scholar Dr. Roger Stritmatter wrote of this:

> "You start to wonder well why do Hamlet and Ophelia have this messed up relationship, well guess what? That messed up relationship comes right out of the lived experience that is documented in Oxford's life. Only someone who is over-educated in English literature would fail to understand the nature of the political problem that is presented by that reality. Anybody on the street can understand that. You have to have a Ph.D. to not get it."

"Witness how greatly thou dost excel in letters. Thine eyes flash fire. Thy countenance shakes a spear!" -- Gabriel Harvey, fellow Cambridge scholar, addressing Edward de Vere (1578).

In more than 50% of the original references to the playwright his name is hyphenated: Shake-speare — an obvious pen name.

Joshua Gray

I SEE A BASTARD
Katherine

My half-brother Edward:
I am suing you. I feel
you are a bastard.

I believe our father
married Margery while
still married to my mother.

Prove me wrong.
I also sue Mary my half-sister.
If I win, you shall be disgraced.

Ashamed. Embarrassed.
Peers will treat you with disrespect.
Their faces red with hatred.

I am hoping
you will lose your nobility.
Good luck.

The Life and Death of King Edward

WEEKS LATER
Edward

I win. You lose. No bastard here!
Now I stick out my tongue,
and spit red raspberries.

Joshua Gray

MY OWN DAUGHTER
William

Ed, we must talk.

> *[Oh God.]*

You are plenty old enough for marriage.
I am going to marry you to Anne.

> *What??!!*

She is red and ready.
You both are to be wed.
The preparations are underway.

You cannot refuse her.
You are a ward of the Court
and I am its guardian.

My sole interest is that my grandkids
have direct ties to the red throne. Politically,
you are that access.

> *Your daughter is*
> *so much a sister.*
> *I will **not** bed her.*

BED TRICK
Anne

I am sorry, Ed, to have set you up.
I am pregnant.
Please, do not reject our child.

You have to admit, it took
smarts, creativity, passion, cunning
to pull off the bed trick.

We are so alike.

I know you hate being married to me
more than you hate me.
I feel married to my brother.

We are the same.

I am married, but I have no husband.
You think you are punishing Father:
You are not. I did nothing, yet I have nothing.

I need someone to eat breakfast with,
to cuddle me up to the red fire,
and talk to me. Please.

Joshua Gray

MY DEAREST ANNE
Edward

I remember sending you little love notes.
Or, more correctly, you have reminded
me of them. I wrote those when I first came

to Cecil House. You were not a sister then.
You were a toddler with a toddler crush.
I humored you. Only time
created a kindred between us.

I adore you as a sister. I may even love you
As such. But I do not love you as a wife.
I am sure you share similar feelings.

I am father to no child. Time will tell
if I forgive you.

I see you as fair. Your red cheeks tell me so.
But are you honest? No. You are not.
You are no virgin.

Get thee to a nunnery.
The years may prove that I love you.
No, I love you not.

The Life and Death of King Edward

FROBISHER'S EXPEDITION OF 1576
Edward

Undad, I hope you loved your vacation.

I lost 3000 pounds, lost
in Frobisher's gamble.

I imagine
Her Majesty spoke
of its outcome.

No? It slipped her mind?

He took three ships to the New World
with a promise of gold.
I went into bond with Lock.

The red ship
never penetrated
the ice. They said the others sank.

I became depressed.

Then the ships returned!
But, it was fool's gold.
Idiot.

Joshua Gray

SHAKES-SPEARE'S RENAISSANCE
Edward

Yes, that is what I said.
I can create an entire culture
England has never known.

How, exactly?

You would be amazed
At Italy's culture,
called The Renaissance.

It would not look good
On England -- or you --
to be so far behind.

Its theater is too advanced
for prose.

I will take us high
Into the greatness of Italy.
I can even improve it

with my words.
Some compare my poetry
to Athena's spear-shaking.

*There is one significant
problem.*

Nobility is shunned
from theatrics. Those comparisons?
They lead to a pen name.

The Life and Death of King Edward

SPENDTHRIFT TYMON
William

I am lost
with what to do
about your money management.

You allow a servant
to give ten pounds to a beggar
while your train holds at the platform.

You financed the building of the Globe.
You created Fisher's Folly
and financed its success
so artists can gather and create together.

You give money to these lewd gentlemen
so they can pay their debts.
Nobilities neither fund nor care for art.

Then there was the time you were attacked
by pirates, left naked, your coins taken.
All because you took no care
arriving from France.

I bet you are in debt with your landlady.
Not to mention your tab at her bar.
Or your special creativity playground.

You have become that Athenian rich fellow.
You will become misanthropic and angry.
I warn you.

Joshua Gray

YOU *MUST* BE A BASTARD
Katherine

Edward, I am suing you once more.
I know you are a bastard;
I have better lawyers.

I was wrong to say you are
the bastard of Earl John.
It is someone else.

I will discover the truth.
Be prepared to be found guilty.
Be prepared to forfeit your life.

I am having fun
proving you wrong.
Edward, here I come.

The Life and Death of King Edward

THE BIGGEST QUERY OF MY LIFE
Edward

My dear Sir, I am wondering if I can ask you
something I hope you will shed light on.
It regards my parentage.

Katherine sued me once, and I won.
I thought nothing of it.
Katherine sued me twice, I lost.

I never questioned anything.
But I became confused. So if
you know anything, tell me.

                                 You are a bastard.

Hell on Horses!

                                 But you are not
                                   the bastard
                               you think you are.

Okay…

                                     Can I speak
                                  as the narrator
                                   of this poem?

Yes.

You were not born in 1550 but '48.
Edward, look at your red hair.
Your mother is The Queen of England.

Joshua Gray

The Life and Death of King Edward

ACT III
(1574 to 1586)

Background Notes

In August 1574 there is a confrontation between Oxford and Queen Elizabeth at the city of Bath, a loud argument. Everyone hears it, but no one knows exactly what they heard. Oxford flees to the continent but shortly thereafter returns.

Oxford reconciles with his wife Anne in 1581-82, after he himself was imprisoned in the Tower by Queen Elizabeth for his affair with Anne Vavasour.

While Oxford's trip to Italy in 1575-1576 was all about experiencing the Renaissance and its art, it also involved learning about the role of art in discussing religion and politics, Catholics and Catholicism, and then later Spain and Catholicism, and impending war. Italy's "Commedia dell' Arte" would prove to be a useful new tool in the evolution of theatre as a public forum and the use of satire to talk about controversial issues.

In June 1586 Oxford was granted (by the Crown) an annuity of £1,000. No accounting of what it was for was ever to be asked or required of him. Was it to write patriotic plays in support of England as Catholic Spain threatened? Some think so. It was, at the very least, highly unusual. The annuity continued throughout his life, and was renewed after the Queen's death in 1603.

The Rev. John Ward, a parish Vicar in Stratford-upon-Avon, wrote in his diary in the 1660s: "Shakespeare had supplied the stage with two plays every year and for that had an allowance so large that he spent at the rate of a thousand pounds a year."

Joshua Gray

Related Plays: Richard II, Henry IV Part 1, Henry IV Part 2, Henry V, Twelfth Night, As You Like It, The Italian Plays

BENVOLIO: Where, underneath the grove of sycamore
That westward rooteth from the city's side,
So early walking did I see your son:"
— *Romeo and Juliet*, I.i.

ESCALUS: You Capulet; shall go along with me:
And, Montague, come you this afternoon,
To know our further pleasure in this case,
To old Free-town, our common judgment-place.
—*Romeo and Juliet*, I.i.

> These are just two of many lines of Shakespeare where the details of Italian landscapes, cultures and local phrases are correctly used. Shaksper didn't go to Italy. Oxford did.

HAMLET: Alas, poor Yorick! I knew him, Horatio; a fellow of infinite jest, of most excellent fancy.
— *Hamlet*, V.i.176

CELIA: you'll be whipped for taxation one of these days.
TOUCHSTONE: The more pity, that fools may not speak wisely what wise men do foolishly.
— *As You Like It*, I.ii.

> "The Shakespearean fool, that highly individual and arresting figure, is no quaint anachronism from the courts of medieval kings, but a highly sophisticated truth-teller. He is a fool *because he tells the truth*. ...

> "If Shakespeare did indeed invent human personality as we know it today, as Harold Bloom has claimed, it says much about the narcissism and self-alienation of modern man." — Charles Beauclerk, *Shakespeare's Lost Kingdom*

JAQUES: I can suck melancholy out of a song, as a weasel sucks eggs. — *As You Like It*,II.v.

> This line is more likely said by a fool than a nobleman. I believe Jaques is a want-to-be fool. Or, at

The Life and Death of King Edward

least, enjoys playing the fool. He is known as melancholic — only a fool would be known so because melancholy can describe an ordinary man. He gets excited by meeting a real, motley fool because in a way that is his aspiration. His monologue on the stages of life should mostly be read as humorous; only the final part gets dramatic, which is why he is again called melancholic.

LAUNCELOT GOBBO: It is a wise father that knows his own child. Well, old man, I will tell you news of your son: give me your blessing: truth will come to light; murder cannot be hid long; a man's son may, but at the length truth will out. —
Merchant of Venice, II.2.77.

HENRY IV: Now, by my sceptre and my soul to boot,
He hath more worthy interest to the state
Than thou the shadow of succession;
— *King Henry IV Part 1*, III.ii.

HENRY IV: God knows, my son,
By what by-paths and indirect crook'd ways
I met this crown; and I myself know well
How troublesome it sat upon my head.
— *King Henry IV Part 2*, IV.v

HENRY V: I tell thee truly, herald,
I know not if the day be ours or no;
For yet a many of your horsemen peer
And gallop o'er the field.
MONTJOY: The day is yours.
— *King Henry V*, IV.vii.

Joshua Gray

A ONE-SIDED CONVERSATION IN BATH
Elizabeth

Eddie, thank you for coming
straightaway to Bath from France
while I vacation.

We flirted through many moons
and fucked more than once.
No one discovered us.

William always knew, of course.

He was there when we decided
a mother and a son could fuck,
since we did not think each other as such.

But I will tell you.
Just after you left for France,
I gave birth to a boy.

I will answer your hazel eyes.
It is yours. I gave him to William.
I will not look upon his red kiwi-hair.

I have done this before, many years ago.
1548. But I am told you were born in 1550.
And *your* red hair comes from a grandmother.

But do not think I have not noticed

your new signature: a crown at the top,
seven slashes at the bottom. Edward VII:
That is what you would be as my successor.

It is treason, you know.
Do not worry.
I find no treason in you.

But if ever there is,
your signature is enough
to stain a rope red.

Figure 7 - Edward de Vere's "Crown" signature

Joshua Gray

SEVEN ITALIAN TOWNS AND MEMORIES THEREOF
Edward

Tell me about Italy.

So many Sycamores along Verona's
westward wall. Villafranca (freetown),
a two-to-three-hour ride.
Saint Peters Church. Saint Francis Monastery,
her crypt in its dungeon.

The boat ride to Milan,
the canal's tide.
Getting off the boats at canal roads.
St. Gregory's well and Il Lazzaretto
are full of corpses.

Saint Luke's parish church in Padua.
A respectable hostel
sits in front of a canal road.
The ride from Pisa
down the Lombardy canal.

The Red Bank of Venice, the penthouse
beside it, both within the Jews' ghetto.
Ah, I loved the rialto! That fascinating Tranect,
pulling boats into Venice. I feel awful
about the way women in Venice live.

The red-walled Sabbioneta, Little Athens
they call it. Their Duke loves the theater.
A quaint tiny temple. Dukes Oak
is not a tree but a small room above its gate.

The Life and Death of King Edward

They call Florence's Piazza The Port.
All Saints Church,
Saint Francis Pilgrim's Hostel
further down the road. *Beautiful Duomo!*
Michelangelo's stunning second Pieta inside.

Vulcano, that magical island of caves
where sounds and voices fill the air.
A large mud pool. Sulphur, gases blowing.
Such yellow sand. Vulcancello!
The island's little valley of monsters.

Joshua Gray

THE CATHOLIC AMONG PROTESTANTS
Edward

> *You visited*
> *Quite a few Italian*
> *Catholic churches.*

Liz, my dear, I will be your servant forever.
I will never be traitor to your crown.
But I was raised Catholic. It is in my blood.

It will take time to find your Protestantism.

I did not go to Italy's south-eastern coast.
I love the Illyrian Mythology;
there were tribes there.

O, to write a comedy of ancient Illyria!

The Life and Death of King Edward

SPAIN THREATENS
Elizabeth

And now, Eddie, a final word
Before we are in London.
I have a job for you.

I believe in the next decade
Or a few years more
Spain will attack England.

We prepare for war,
But should Spain strike tomorrow
England falls.

Spain grows fear in us.
Their armada may be huge.

> *Where am I*
> *in this?*

We must build our navy
and not our people.
They will grow suspicious
of the crown.

I must hire your words.
Write a prosperous
history of England.

Bring me your Italian Renaissance.
Start with comedy. When there is struggle,
write your histories.

I shall pay you well and regularly.

Joshua Gray

THE FOOL IS A TRUTH-TELLER
Elizabeth

Eddie, you must know I prefer
talking to you about your plays
when the others have left.

> *I noticed.*

And so, I want to tell you
what I believe I have discovered
about your fool: he is the truth-teller.

> *Exactly!*

In *Twelfth Night, or What You Will*
Feste the Clown is more of one

> *[That's not his all!]*

than Touchstone in *As You Like It*,
though Jaques might be Feste's equal!

But I believe your fools will improve as
time goes on. As truth-tellers, that is.
Maybe dramatic plays will show them off.

> *You might be right...*

The Life and Death of King Edward

THE FIRST HENRY TETRALOGY
Elizabeth

My dear Eddie, let me get this straight.

Richard II was me,
and Bolingbroke Spain.
This is the worst scenario. Then,

Prince Hal was you
with all your drunk artists
and Henry IV was William.

Are you saying William
is my usurper or your father?

John Falstaff:
a foolish William in the first
and a foolish you in the second.

Furthermore I am Henry IV
in Part 2. You are saying
you can forget foolishness.

The judge. Fuck!
The judge is William.

Henry V, you prove to me
You can be King Edward VII,
my successful successor.

How did I do?

Not bad. Not bad at all.

Joshua Gray

REUNITED WITH ANNE
Edward

I am most cruel.
No. I accept your child.
As my own. And if you want me,

I allow you into my blood red bed;
No more need for bed tricks.
I want to be your loving husband.

> *O...my...god....yes!*

I am *happy*!

O and can you tell me, who is
The red-headed boy
now living with Undad?

> *He is the 3rd Earl*
> *of Southampton:*
> *Henry Wriothesley.*

The Life and Death of King Edward

ACT IV
(1587 to 1603)

Background Notes

In 1593 "William Shake-speare" bursts upon the scene in London, first with epic poems, and then with plays. These works were mainly about succession, and oaths, and duty, and bastards.

Also during the 1590s there developed what historians have called the "Succession Crisis," so named since Queen Elizabeth refused to name a successor, and forbid any public discussion of the succession issue.

Many writers during the 1590s ran afoul of the censors and State power. Some were arrested and tortured, some died. In 1599 the "Bishop's Fire" was a public burning of all banned books and pamphlets. Nothing by Shakespeare was ever banned or burned in the 1590s.

In 1601 the Essex Rebellion sought to determine who controlled the succession question, and perhaps even who should be the successor to Elizabeth. Shakespeare's Richard II was performed for the conspirators the night before. Many were arrested and punished. Six were executed. Shakespeare was not arrested, or even questioned. Henry Wriothesley, condemned to death for his role in the rebellion, was not executed.

In 1603 Queen Elizabeth died. Henry Wriothesley was released from prison and granted a full pardon. Throughout these years Oxford was in retirement and absent from court. He died in 1604 and his passing was not publicly noted, nor was there a funeral, nor even a will. The whereabouts of his burial place remains unknown to this day.

Joshua Gray

*Related Plays: Hamlet, Much Ado About Nothing,
Twelfth Night Troilus and Cressida, Henry IV Part 1,
King John Coriolanus, Hamlet, King Lear, The Tempest*

COUNTESS: In delivering my son from me, I bury
a second husband. -- *All's Well That Ends Well*, I.i.1

BENEDICK: Two of them have the very bent of
        honour;
And if their wisdoms be misled in this,
The practise of it lives in John the bastard,
Whose spirits toil in frame of villanies.
—*Much Ado About Nothing*, IV.i.

CLOWN: Thou hast spoke for us, madonna, as if
thy eldest son should be a fool; whose skull Jove
cram with Brains! — *Twelfth Night*, I.v.112.

> Notice how 'madonna' is uncapitalized. That and his
> line above tells us Feste the clown is Olivia's son.

THERSITES: I am a bastard too; I love bastards: I
        am a bastard
begot, bastard instructed, bastard in mind, bastard
in valour, in every thing illegitimate. One bear will
not bite another, and wherefore should one
        bastard?
Take heed, the quarrel's most ominous to us: if the
son of a whore fight for a whore, he tempts
        judgment:
farewell, bastard. —*Troilus and Cressida*, V.vii.

BASTARD: I am I, howe'er I was begot.
—*King John*, I.i.

> The natural order of succession states that the King's
> eldest son takes the throne; but in *Hamlet*, the title
> character remains a Prince. Why? Elizabethans
> would have understood that Hamlet is a bastard
> child.

POLONIUS: And that your grace hath screen'd and
stood between/Much heat and him." -- To
Gertrude, about Hamlet.

> Hamlet's first and last lines are 1 and 7 lines long,
> respectively. Edward was Oxford's 17th Earl.

The Life and Death of King Edward

> On at least one occasion, Elizabeth I called Edward de Vere, "My little bastard."

EDMUND: For that I am some twelve or fourteen moonshines
Lag of a brother? Why 'bastard?' Wherefore 'base,'
When my dimensions are as well compact,
My mind as generous and my shape as true
As honest madam's issue? Why brand they us
With 'base,' with 'baseness,' 'bastardy,' 'base,' 'base,'
Who, in the lusty stealth of nature, take
More composition and fierce quality
Than doth, within a dull, stale, tired bed
Go to th' creating a whole tribe of fops
Got 'tween asleep and wake?

Now, gods, stand up for bastards! — *King Lear*, I.ii.

> King Lear had three daughters. One of them was a favorite. So too did Edward de Vere.

PROSPERO: And deeper than did ever plummet sound
I'll drown my book. — *The Tempest.* (V.i).

And thence retire me to my Milan, where
Every third thought shall be my grave. — *The Tempest*, (V.i).

> Richard Roe (*The Shakespeare Guide to Italy*) notes that, "We can strongly suspect that the departure-from-Milan was a 'doctoring' of the original manuscript by high authority..." Roe's argument is that the city was most likely Venice, but politics at the time forbade its mention, though at the 2016 Shakespeare Oxford Fellowship conference it was reported that there was a canal route from Milan to the western shore.

"I am Richard II, know ye not that?" — Queen Elizabeth, speaking to historian William Lambarde, several months after the Essex Rebellion.

"In this common shipwreck mine is above all the rest..." — A letter from Oxford to Robert Cecil, dated April 24/25, 1603, the evening before the burial of Queen Elizabeth.

.

Joshua Gray

A LETTER TO HORACE
Edward

Do you know you are the same age
as I was when I left home?
That was so long ago.

I hear you desire to play
with someone's Fool.
Next time you are in London,
I shall give you my Fool for the day.

He will be committed to you.
I remember my father's acting troupe.
They stayed with us during Winter:

one of them was a retired fool!
I believe he was the Queen's father's jester.
O! He had such *infinite jest*! Gave me

who-knows-how-many piggy back rides!
You would have loved him, Horace!
I promise. The next time we see each other.

The Life and Death of King Edward

YOU WRONG ME
Elizabeth

Mister, You hath done me much wrong.

> *Have I,*
> *Elizabeth? No.*

You look on me with disgust
at my advances, answer me
with silence.

I have done nothing
to you, merely allowed you
my nothing.

You no longer have the privilege
to name me Liz; should you speak again,
use formalities.

I will continue to discuss your plays,
and at those times I command you to speak.

> *Your Majesty,*
> *I speak to you*
> *through my plays.*

> *But I shall speak*
> *to you again.*

Joshua Gray

CODE WORDS
Edward

Your Majesty, since you do not
want me
to call you Liz, I will refer to us

in my plays: I am truth and worms,
for that is *mon nom* en Francais.
You are fair, because of your hair.

But if I speak of my bastard,
he is fair
and you are beauty.

I speak of myself also
as n/ever or every, for E. ver is my name.
O, not Oh, the same.

Do not worry. These are common words.
O they will never get the truth
of my fair and beauteous words.

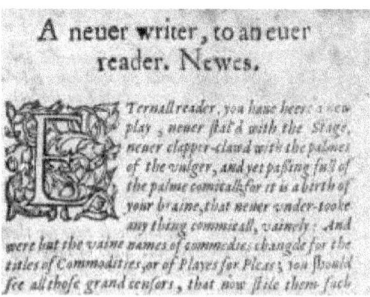

Figure 8 - From Troilus and
Cressida, 1609 quarto:
"A never writer, to an ever
reader. Newes."

The Life and Death of King Edward

MUCH ADO ABOUT THE BASTARD
Elizabeth

My dearest Eddie, why, you gave me
the most succulent character
in this new comedy of yours. I love Beatrice.

> *But what
> of John?*

John? A cruel man! Why even ask?
He hates being the bastard.
And wants everyone to pay.

He has notoriously nothing friends,
who help him with his evil pranks.
I want none of him.

Nothing is worse than
ruining a true love and proper wedding:
convince the groom his bride a whore.

John the bastard has no honor.

Joshua Gray

WIDE AWAKE AFTERWARDS
Edward

Welcome to the Globe, Henry.
I am happy you want to act!
I shall put you in the good roles
and Mentor you.
O what fun we shall have!

As an aside,
has anyone told you
I am your father?

Time...*To sleep, perchance to dream*
and come back to reality.

But to act with the bastard is beet!

The Life and Death of King Edward

THE BASTARD
Edward

Why do I love the bastard so?

I developed Philip out of warmth.

John the Bastard was mean. Insecure. Cold.
He saw the world as if his life was judgment.
But *he* owned the grudge.

Philip is John's opposite. Philip denied
he was a bastard,
yet never cared being one. He was overjoyed
to discover Coeur de Lion was his blood.

He was optimistic, served his King.
His character filled several roles:
a King's fool, a truth-teller, bastard-Prince,
Narrator, stand-up comic.

That I gave him the final lines
indicates his importance.

You love him simply because he is one
of my histories' most loveable.

Joshua Gray

ELIZABETH THINKS AS SHE PACES
Elizabeth

On my left, Volumnia is a fool.
She controls her son, wants him
to be what *she* desires. He should be
all he can be: a damn good soldier.

On my right, Coriolanus is a fool.
While Edward never states explicitly, it seems
Coriolanus is a bastard.

The crowd would not hate a legitimate!
A poor-mannered man is merely disliked.
She wants him to be great perhaps to prove
a bastard can be so.

Only a bastard could be so angry
that he would leave town
to win the pride of thieves.

(Timon also became a misanthrope,
though he wasn't a bastard.
Edward is a bit misanthropic, though.

After all, Edward was found
to be a bastard. My little bastard.)

Then there is the bastard Hamlet.
A poor boy takes the throne
should he be legitimate.

Gertrude is not very sensible.
There is an incestuous relationship
between her and Hamlet.

The Life and Death of King Edward

The scene in her closet proves it.

Is Edward telling me I'm his mother?
But he was born later.
I'd chop off William's head if it were so.

No, I would not. I will not
be my father.

Gertrude is an aloof lady.
Am I aloof too?

Joshua Gray

EDGAR/EDWARD/EDMUND
Edward

What did I like about writing
Edgar and Edmund? Elizabeth
are you nuts?

> *No. But don't forget your formalities.*

The names, of course.
Both of their names start with Ed.
So does mine.

If Edgar is the good legitimate son,
and Edmund is the evil bastard son,
Then I am a mix of the two.

I am a bastard,
but I am a good bastard,
Thus both of them make up me.

Figure 9 - Minerva Britanna *(1612) title page. The partially hidden hand is writing a phrase in Latin ("MENTE VIDE BOR [I]"), an anagram for "TIBI NOM. DE VERE"*

The Life and Death of King Edward

ESSEX REBELLION
Edward

> *I should have said,*
> *this goes nowhere.*

I knew so, Henry, from your request.

You do know it is treason,
what you and Essex are planning.
You ask me to commit treason too,

even if it is not against the Queen.
Robert is my foster brother.
Though we never felt it.

I will
not partake in it myself.
Find another actor.
Using my play alone is death.

I will not be questioned.

Yes. You may put on Richard the Second
when you confront Robert with arms
and demand to know the Queen's successor.

But do me one favor:
use the deposition scene.

Know you will die.

Joshua Gray

SURREAL
Edward

Robert, sir, I have always been in your debt.
Your kindness is much appreciated.
I grieve tremendously for the mistress lost.
In this common shipwreck, mine
is above all the rest.

Though I went out of her favor decades ago,
I cared about her deeply throughout.
She fell into such dementia!

She discovered our truth years ago, I believe.
Perhaps she asked your father.

I worry about my plays. I worry
future generations will think
that stupid Stratford man
is the author of my life.

Plays are not the places
to write dedications. Poems are.
I digress.

How were you in these last days?
How are you now?
Tell me your heart.

I hope my portrayal of Richard the Third
did not spark an endless grudge.

As Ever, Your Pawn. Or your Rook.

The Life and Death of King Edward

ACT V
(1590 to 1603)

The Sonnets

Background Notes

SHAKE-SPEARES SONNETS, *the sequence of numbered verses printed in 1609, has been referred to as the greatest puzzle in the history of English literature. This artistic masterwork has thrilled and moved millions of readers for centuries, but the verses have also been an enigma in terms of their meaning, as well as their relationship to the author's life and contemporary history.*

But the Oxfordian theory of Shakespeare has provided a window into their true meaning, most recently through the work of Oxfordian author/researcher Hank Whittemore who, in The Monument (2005), *identified the historical context as primarily the circumstances surrounding the Essex Rebellion of 1601 and the question of who would succeed Queen Elizabeth on the English throne. This new way of reading the Sonnets brings them alive as a true story of political intrigue, passion, and betrayal. Ultimately, they portray the end of the Tudor dynasty as recorded in a clandestine diary.*

In this political-historical interpretation of the verses the Poet is Edward de Vere, 17th Earl of Oxford, the Fair Youth is Henry Wriosthesley, 3rd Earl of Southampton, and the Dark Lady is Queen Elizabeth. The time period begins in the early 1590s and ends with the death of Elizabeth in 1603. This new historical context is confirmed in the Sonnets by specific, recorded events surrounding

Joshua Gray

Southampton's imprisonment (1601-1603) and release (1603). Further, when studied from the standpoint of their structure, the 100 sonnets at the center (27-126) support the conclusion that the author had deliberately erected a "monument" of verse for Henry Wriosthesley, to whom he promised "all happiness and eternity."

In the following pages each sonnet has been reduced to a quatrain and the language modernized. Hank Whittemore has generously provided compressed versions of his original notes on each "chapter" of the sonnets in order to illustrate the underlying storyline and structure.

"Well, it turns out that the whole story is right there in front of us in this one monument of sonnets. He's adding the truth that you're not going to learn in the history books." – Hank Whittemore, *Last Will. and Testament*

"If by identifying Shakespeare as Oxford, and you're gradually led into identifying Southampton as his and Elizabeth's son, what your doing is, you're entering into the question of who is the rightful sovereign of Britain, then you've *got* to keep Oxford's authorship of Shakespeare unknown, because this involves the succession to the British throne. I mean this is powerful stuff!" – Charlton Ogburn, Jr., *Last Will. and Testament*

Author's Note:

I originally reduced *Shake-speares Sonnets* to quatrains over a two-month period in 2015 and tweeted them using the #bard154 hashtag.

The sonnets here are slightly expanded from the 140 characters on Twitter, to allow for punctuation and proper spelling of names.

The Life and Death of King Edward

DEDICATION AND PROLOGUE

Dedication: To the only reason
for these sonnets, Mr. [Wriothesley, Henry]
all happiness and eternity promised
by our [E.Ver] living poet.

153.
Diana's maid found poor Cupid
And buried his blood in a cold lake.
It borrowed fire to heat its waters.
Only Diana can save him.

Joshua Gray

THE FIRST 26
Edward to Henry

"LORD OF MY LOVE"
THE FAIR YOUTH (1-26)

THE MARRIAGE PROPOSAL (1-17)
1591 (Representing Henry's 17 Years)

Edward de Vere urges his royal bastard son, Henry Wriothesley, to perpetuate his bloodline by begetting a legitimate heir by marriage. At the same time, William Cecil is pressuring Henry to marry his granddaughter, Elizabeth Vere, who is Edward's reputed daughter – a deal that, if Henry succeeded the Queen, would elevate the Cecil family to the status of royalty. Is this the condition under which Cecil would support the Queen in naming Henry as the future Henry IX of England?

1.[1]
The Queen and I desired an heir
For her bloodline's survival.
But you, son, refuse your name.
Pity England has you.

2.
When you're old, your own fortune refused,
unable to give royal answer,
You'll wish to say, Look at my heir!
Wouldn't that be great?

3.
Same old face in your mirror.
What if it were someone new?
You're too much like your mother.
Act! Or your royal-ness dissolves...

---
[1] William Cecil wants a wedding between his granddaughter and Wriothesley, who could become heir to the throne. But the earl refuses to marry. In Sonnets 1-17, Edward de Vere tries to convince Wriothesley to marry.

The Life and Death of King Edward

4.
My wasteful son,
Your mother merely lends her line.
Why abuse your ancestry
Yet take it to the grave?

5.
The Queen who birthed you
destroys you. Her blood deprived,
Hope diminished. Though as
Roses die, their buds live.

6.
Therefore make babies! Sex
and more sex to make
ten to one-hundred times yourself!
Selfish child, do not die without a child.

7.
Look, Princes are loved
in youth and in age. But near-death,
the people set eyes for a new Lord.
If you want fame, have a son.

8.
As love only attracts love,
why be offended of affections?
The Queen and I do swear: to die
with no heir is your royal line's death.

9.
Does fear you'll make a widow
keep you single? England is your widow
if you waste your blood on no one.
You disgrace only yourself.

10.
For shame! You kill, not save,
your mother's name! Change course
and be the King you are.
Do it for me, let royal blood live past you.

11.
A name wanes fast, as fast
A son's name lasts. Let others die
Nameless. Your mother meant
You should print her seal.

12.
When I watch your aging mother
When I hear of greatness lost
Then I question your royal loyalty.
Only an heir can make you King.

13.
Know your bloodline owns you,
That your royal claim is borrowed,
If bought, a son would buy again.
I'm your father, you are whose?

14.
I study the stars not to gain luck
nor to help princes in war. I read
them to see how your fall means
your parents' death.

15.
People & plants have but a moment
of perfection, but you're ever-rich
in my eyes, even in crisis.
I fight for your place!

The Life and Death of King Edward

16.
Why fight against your royalty
It's time to bear the royal rose
and deflower the lady in question.
A son quite guarantees a rose.

17.
Heaven knows my rhyme
holds your grave. Cite your royalty
and I'm called a liar. But an heir
makes two of you: you, and my rhyme.

THE SHAKESPEARE COMMITMENT (18-26)
(1592-1600, one sonnet per year)

Henry has rejected the marriage proposal, but Edward continues to support him. Soon, in 1593, he publishes under the "Shakespeare" pen name, dedicating two narrative poems to Henry and declaring, "The love I dedicate to your Lordship is without end ... What I have done is yours, what I have to do is yours." In other words, he has adopted the Shakespeare mask in order to publicly support his royal son – who joins forces with the Earl of Essex against the power of William Cecil and his son, Robert Cecil, to control the eventual succession to Queen Elizabeth

18.[2]
A Child of the Tudor line finds
life hard. Your eternal flame
will not be lost as long as I rhyme.
As breath gives life, you give words.

---

[2] Starting with Sonnet 18: Wriothesley refused all matchmaking efforts and lost Burghley's support. Edward writes his bastard son a sonnet per year for the next nine years (1592-1600).

19.
Time, kill the Queen, her line,
Be sorrow & joy as seasons fade.
But don't steal my son, yet do your best:
He lives within my rhyme.

20.
A false Queen's heart feels
coming-of-age prides a mother.
With your birth I lost a crown --
your blood is her joy!

21.
It is you, not I, who inspires
songs of royal blood.
My commitment to you is strong!
I will not sell your words of history.

22.
My youth ages and dies only if
the Queen names another.
Be careful and support your line:
loyalty to me cannot make you royalty.

23.
Like a prideful actor forgetting lines
I sit in fear of royalty's might.
Let my songs lead with light
and listen to the unspoken!

24.
I paint you and your mother's blood,
see my skill in telling truths!
Your eyes are my windows.
Blind eyes cannot see your royalty.

The Life and Death of King Edward

25.
Unlike many I don't boast to know
the Queen's blood.
Her favorites lose their footing; I'm happy
to have a son, disgraced by war.

26.[3]
Royal son, our strong bond
is silent. I cannot go public:
until you have the Crown,
neither one can acknowledge the other.

---

[3] 26 is the envoy ending this sequence, which represents 26 years of Wriothesley's life. Tensions before the Essex Rebellion are high, and he wants to break the stronghold on the crown's successor.

Joshua Gray

THE FIRST 50 OF THE MIDDLE 100
Edward to Henry

THE CRIME (27-36)
February 8 – 17, 1601

Upon the failed rebellion of February 8, 1601, Henry is taken to the Tower of London where he and Essex face charges of high treason and near-certain execution. Edward will mark each day with one sonnet until his son is either executed or reprieved. Now he is summoned to the "sessions" or trial to sit on the tribunal, which will be forced to render a guilty verdict. Edward pledges his legal support behind the scenes: "Thy adverse party is thy Advocate." (35)

27.[4]
What a day. I'm exhausted.
But my thoughts go to you, the Tower.
I see your princely shadow there.
At night, for you, there is no rest.

28.
I can't be happy if I can't rest.
Day, night both torture me.
I tell day you're royal, flatter night.
Day saddens as night is hope.

29.
You've lost true blood, I my own name.
I want words known, kings free
from high prison. I will not change
views on succession.

---

[4] The center 100 sonnets can be divided into ten chapters:
Sonnets 27-36: The crime
The Essex Rebellion has failed. Henry Wriothesley is imprisoned in the Tower of London. A heavy dark time.

The Life and Death of King Edward

30.
I'll pay my fatherly dues again;
can I cry for you, disgraced,
from sad price to sad price:
once at my royal death, now at yours.

31.
You are most royal by blood,
I've shed many tears for your royal right.
You are your own royal grave.
Know you're everything to me.

32.
If you escape death & Elizabeth
hears me, lets me write again,
think my muse grew your name,
& my name's death was a poet's gift.

33.
Many mornings you've flattered
mountains, the Dark Queen clouded
your claim from England. An hour mine,
still I do not disdain you.

34.
Royal promise is so disloyal!
Eased pain can't ease disgrace.
You repent yet I'm unrelieved.
Crime's tears require poet's ransom.

35.
Clouds stain both mother and son.
My plays author-ized your deed.
I advocate for you, find you guilty.
I accomplice you who rob me.

36.
I'll testify to separate us two
& rob royal succession for good:
publicly you are not my son;
yet privately, my song is your truth.

THE TRIAL (37-46)
February 18 – 27, 1601

The trial is held on February 19, 1601 and both earls are found guilty and sentence to death. Essex is beheaded six days later, but Henry remains in the Tower and his fate continues to be uncertain.

37.[5]
Your mother's disgust lames me,
but cannot rob my love for you.
To fuse you within my words
Does not lame, but makes me most happy.

38.
Dead muses can't exist while you live.
No man is mute while you inspire.
Your muse is best;
My pained, weak muse sees your glory.

39.
My lowly self praises you high!
Our ties cut, my song is quiet.
Your freedom could yield no thoughts,
so your life is twice-felt.

---

[5] Sonnets 37-46: The Trial
Edward, highest-ranking earl, is forced to sentence his son to death, and tries to save him with his sonnets.

The Life and Death of King Edward

40.
Take all royalty you've given,
you still have none. Is there blame?
I forgive you for robbing your name
from me. I'm your ally!

41.
Temptation moves in my absence.
What Queen's son acts so common?
Do not, imprisoned, attempt the crown
by announcing double truths.

42.
Your mother's a Dark Lady!
You serve since I serve. I lose you,
& you her, you live. I've lost you both!
As we are one, she has two.

43.
Day, dis-grace; night, a Grace:
a mother's stain makes royal might
while I dream. The days I wait
for you; nights you wait on me.[6]

44.
My deadened flesh is thoughts of me
outside a tower and then within.
But thought does not make it so.
In slow time, we grieve.

---

[6] Between sonnets 43 and 44 Essex, Wriothesley's co-conspirator, is executed.

45.
Air & fire confine, move thoughts, desire.
My deathly life sank until
your illness turned royal health,
which again saddens me.

46.
My eye & heart are at war:
Do you live in a heart or a tower?
Heart's thought decides Eye's sight.
Eye sees skin; heart sees blood.

THE PLEA (47-56)
February 28 – March 9, 1601

Edward vows to create "the living record" of his royal son for posterity, by means of these sonnets – if the "monument" can escape government suppression. Meanwhile he is pleading with the Queen and Cecil for some way to save Henry from execution.

47.[7]
My heart, my eye agree to help
each other contains you.
Though imprisoned you stay with me.
Sleeping senses rise at your image!

48.
My songs stay quiet for your truth,
but you are prey to death.
I didn't lock you in towers, but hearts:
where you will be stolen.

---

[7] Sonnets 47-56: The Plea.
Edward and Robert bargain: Wriothesley is spared from death but cannot claim to be his mother's successor.

The Life and Death of King Edward

49.
In worse days you'll see me
responsible, deny my parentage.
I'll swear against me to save you;
The Law will take you away.

50.
I tell of bargains, leave you
heavy on tired horseback.
I ride in anger; it trots in groan.
Grief lies ahead. Joy stands with you.

51.
Leaving you desires no speed.
Returning, I'll ride Diana-high!
What horse keeps up with blood?
I'll run to you without its need.

52.
The royal key brings me to you
sparingly: my Tower visits, rare.
Prison plays you as my coffin.
Covered and free: my blood son.

53.
Your blood casts royal frowns.
My Adonis is poorly you.
The Queen kisses your fresh cheek.
No other royalty is written in eternity.

54.
Royalty made great with my heir.
Disgraced heirs are still heirs --
Tudor heirs summon royalty!
My songs reveal a dead son's truth.

55.
In my songs you reign more royal
than marble busts, ruined by war.
Against oblivion you live!
Until you're known you live in songs.

56.
Stronger than my purpose:
find your former royal strength.
Prison is the ebb and flow of royal duty.
Dark times make golden times.

THE REPRIEVE (57-66)
March 10 – 19, 1601

Edward tries to "fortify" himself (63) against the terrible vision of his son's impending execution. At the last moment, after several others have been "hanged, drawn and quartered" or beheaded, Henry is spared – his sentence quietly (and without official record) commuted to perpetual imprisonment. Relieved, Edward is nonetheless devastated that his son will never be King of England. He writes a suicide note (66), saying he would leave this earth but for the fact he would be leaving Henry "alone" to wither in the Tower.

57.[8]
I, nameless, am your servant.
No bitter complaints about fates.
I think only of your royal service.
I, Edward write your Will.

58.
Servants can't control royal time.
My name patiently suffers
for freedom. Pardon yourself!
A hellish wait can't blame your will.

---

[8] Sonnets 57-66: The Reprieve.
Elizabeth can still void the bargain. Crowds gather for Wriothesley's impending execution. High tension.

The Life and Death of King Edward

59.
My songs birth a bastard son again!
To see you within the history:
do my songs shed light or no?
Older books are dimmer than mine!

60.
Each minute succeeds the other
to your death. She who bears, destroys.
Her dying age devours you.
Will my songs escape her hand?

61.
Do you ask my sleepless nights
to think of you, write of your disgrace?
No. I keep myself awake.
I am your watchman; I see for you.

62.
I'm a narcissist to the bones.
My face is a most Kingly face.
But my mirror shines a different me.
You are me. It is you I love.

63.
I'll stand tall when The Dark Lady
kills you, your succession ruined.
But she can't kill memories;
Your blood lives in my rhyme.

64.
I see your mother destroy mortal
royalty; James of Scotland boards
his ship. The Tudor Rose wilts.
I weep; too soon you'll be lost.[9]

---

[9] Between 64 and 65: During the last several days many people have been executed. Wriothesley appears more lost than [e. ver]. Edward braces for the worst.

65.
Mortal things are meeker than mortality:
how can you survive your fate?
What calms your wrathful mother?
Pray my ink can. It may.

66.[10]
Shall I die? You're nobody,
disgraced, disabled. Your claim
promised to another. My verse
tongue-tied by authority. You're alive!

THE PENANCE (67-76)
March 20 – 29, 1601

Edward stops writing one sonnet to correspond with each day. He records his personal penance on behalf of his son – the forfeiting of any royal claim by Henry and his own permanent obliteration as author of the Shakespeare works: "My name be buried where my body is." (72) He arrives at the very midpoint of the 100-sonnet central sequence (76-77), stating in 76 that his sole subject matter revolves around "all one, ever the same" (Henry = his motto "all one"; Edward = "ever"; and the Queen = her motto "ever the same").

67.[11]
Why must you be imprisoned,
among thieves, falsely displayed?
You are the royal heir. She keeps
you within the Tower as a reminder.

---

[10] Between 65 and 66: Elizabeth spares her son from death and accepts the bargain, to which Wriothesley "the late earl" is committed, his possessions taken. Edward is overjoyed, but also grieves, and in 66 considers suicide.

[11] Sonnets 67-76: The Penance
Wriothesley is now a commoner, spared but still imprisoned. Edward is dimmed, depressed.

The Life and Death of King Edward

68.
You're now a museum piece, alive
to tell stories of royal yester-year.
Through the blood of old kings,
she sets you upon her mantle.

69.
My songs say you're royal.
Cecil admires you; in private
destroys you. Disgrace after praise.
You, now a commoner, cannot grow.

70.
You are a crow, a traitor, a suspect
who strengthens as the Queen ages.
Neither dead nor named,
let us see you, a crime unmasked.

71.
When I'm (perhaps) dead,
I've disappeared instead. Forget
the author of songs. Do not speak of me
but let your blood die with me.

72.
When I die my name won't help you.
Let my name be buried with my body
so one of us disgraces not the other.
We are both ashamed.

73.
I'm old. I saw glamour, see death
of lines. I'm dusk of a royal sky,
coals of a blood fire. I loved
the line that gave you up.

74.
If I die before you're released
review my songs of preserved blood.
I'll've been beaten by cowards!
Blood determined by contents.

75.
I'm conflicted on your life.
Should royal dishonesty keep
secrets from England? Too much
or too little of you is a good thing.

76.[12]
This no-pride center of songs:
all one, ever the same; every word
doth almost tell my name. My son,
new and old, make old words new.

---

[12] 76 is the series' center sonnet. Edward crams it all into 76, & reminds us to read the work in order to identify the author.

The Life and Death of King Edward

THE SECOND 50 OF THE MIDDLE 100
Edward to Henry

THE SACRIFICE AND RIVAL POET (77-86)
March 30 – April 8, 1601

In the second middle sonnet (77), Edward dedicates "this book" to Henry, calling it "thy book" that contains his story. In the rest of this chapter he portrays the sacrifice of his own name to that of his printed pseudonym "Shakespeare," the "other" or so-called rival poet who can praise his son publicly while he himself must be silent.

77.[13]
Your mirror & clock show blood's
demise, your grave, your robbery.
Learn your sad songs; know
their contents: your royal birth.

78.
You offer aid to my foreign name,
teach my mute words to sing.
My muse is my subject, too:
your art is my art, a skill raised high!

79.
My crippled songs, my sick muse
name me. Your case deserves
a better author than he that robs you.
Thank him for what I say!

---

[13] In 76 Edward reminded us he is the author; In 77, also in the center, he reminds us his son Wriothesley is to whom the sonnets are dedicated.

Sonnets 78-86: Rival Poet.
A battle of identity between a man's true self (Edward) and his public pen name (Shake-speare).

80.
My weak hand holds a strong pen.
A boat sails the same as a ship;
You steer him further out to sea;
I stay strong in my muted way.

81.
My songs will sing your truth while
I'm forgotten. You'll be immortal,
I, most mortal. Your monument,
these lines, their breadth.

82.
Read my poems' dedications for
your name, rich in self-color.
Read the rose-cheeked true words
of your ever-true other father.

83.
Private Poet has no need
to inflate fate with Public Poet.
Silent Life writes well-known words,
still too short of such royalty!

84.
Which of me writes more praise of you?
We write of you, me and me, that
you are you. We write and praise you
to hide your curse.

85.
My silent muse thinks well
& my known muse speaks well.
I read his praise & praise my songs.
Respect my well-spoken silence!

86.
Is the tomb of songs your womb?
Did my songs kill me? No:
my songs live. My other, causeless.
One of me sings, the other is mute.

THE TEACHING (87-96)
April 1601 – January 1602)

Edward records for posterity that the Queen has reduced Henry's verdict from "treason" to "misprision" of treason (87), thereby allowing him to be released and given a royal pardon – but only if Robert Cecil brings James of Scotland to the English throne upon Elizabeth's death. Henry is unhappy with this backdoor deal. Even while still in the Tower, he begins to stir others to rebellion; but Edward warms him (96) against it.

87.[14]
Farewell! My royal son. I am severed.
How do I deserve you? Your gifts?
Misprision. Better judgment.
I sleep, you're King, but then I wake.

88.
I'll write to show your blood;
my songs become your story.
I'll gain myself as well!
I belong to you and write your wrongs.

89.
Say I commit a crime, I say it's true.
I'll say I'm a stranger to you,
& not speak of a Henry IX.
I'll argue with me & unclaim you.

---

[14] Sonnets 87-96: The Teaching.
Wriothesley's sentence is officially reduced from execution to continued imprisonment (misprision, a lesser form of treason), paving the way for a pardon.

Joshua Gray

90.
Renounce me, now! I submit.
Do not commit a crime from behind.
Leave me first, and now. Let other
pain feel painless in your light.

91.
Men state their strength,
& go their joyful way, but not me.
You best my strength, & I boast.
I'm wretched; make me wretched still.

92.
You were given life to give you life.
My life ends upon your ending life.
My term dependant on your term.
It's true you're no liar.

93.
I'll live because you're my son.
England writes your false story,
but your mother birthed a royal boy,
even if you can't show it.

94.
Whoever can cause ill change
but won't are just and true.
Do not let another crime take hold.
Sweetness is soured with ill action!

95.
Sweet blood envelopes your bad fame,
& keeps your name raised.
What a tower that turns robbers
to royalty! Still any rebel thought.

The Life and Death of King Edward

96.
Loved is a criminal & a King.
The Queen sees a crime less
than blood. Oh, would-be followers!
Alas, my songs are your strength.

LOST MUSE FOUND (97-106)
February 8, 1602 – April 9, 1603

Edward marks the first "fleeting year" (97) of Henry's imprisonment. The long days and nights stretch on and on, all too slowly, until Edward can barely summon the strength to write to his son. He marks his son's second year in the Tower (104) followed by the Queen's death (105) on March 24, 1603, when James of Scotland is proclaimed King James I of England. Now Edward's muse returns, because he knows Henry will be liberated. Edward then marks Henry's final night in prison (106) on April 9, 1603.

97.[15]
A year past, a death, such dark days:
a Summer, Fall, and a widow's womb.
You're an orphan of a muted man.
We dread She will die.

98.
I write less, as I see you long ago
in her womb. Ruin awaits.
Yet I do not sing of her full term.
Death is a tower, a royal shadow.

99.
A 15-liner, a sad rebuke of you.
A royal thief of one's own belief!
Flowers taken, colors blackened.
Tudor blood curdles for death.

---

[15] Sonnets 97-106: Lost Muse Found
Two "fleeting" years and one month exactly since the rebellion and imprisonment. The tide is bleak and tragic.

100.
My muse left: a dried pen, a fury faint
and dark. Return and enrage me!
Blood dies. Muse, renew it, stop
ruin by a deathly queen.

101.
Welcome, Muse. You've neglected
the queen & me. Answer!
Silence's no excuse; eternity lives in song.
I'll teach you again to write.

102.
Your power gains blood to bargain.
A boy accepted with my songs.
You're no less royal than when
birds sang of a blood turned base.

103.
No-hope Muse, write a line.
Your mirror sees a line I can't write!
It's worse to write boasting lines;
mirror, right you a throne.

104.[16]
You're the same as ever. Thrice
Winter came. Three Aprils, Junes
since I've seen you. Blood dies
upon a bed. Future! Tudor's dead.

---

[16] Between 103 and 104: Elizabeth is now on her deathbed. Three winters have passed since Wriothesley's imprisonment.

The Life and Death of King Edward

105.[17]
No idols have come, only songs.
My child is my blood, all-ways.
You, she and I: spent themes of one
seat sitting alone: all-one.

106.[18]
You'll be a knight among the Wights.
My songs still sing your line.
Other praise sees you with no line,
and we cannot speak truth.

THE QUARREL (107-116)
April 10 – 19, 1603

Edward now resumes his arrangement of one sonnet per day. He will use nineteen sonnets to mark the nineteen days from Henry's release on April 10, 1603 from being "supposed as forfeit to a confined doom" (107) until the Queen's funeral (125) on April 28, 1603, followed by a single envoy (126) to bid "my lovely Boy" farewell. Edward has met with his son, who is still angry over the deal his father made with Cecil; they argue, but Edward writes that their "marriage of true minds" cannot "admit impediments." (116) He praises the glory of Henry's royal blood, which can never be destroyed.

107.[19]
No public fear can control you.
The Queen your mother is dead.
I live in songs; Death retreats from you.
Your monument is my song.

---

[17] 105: 26 months (over 3 winters) since Wriothesley's imprisonment. His motto: One for All, All for One. A month since 104, Elizabeth is dead. 24 March 1603
[18] 106: James VI of Scotland is now King James I, & orders the pardon of Wriothesley. Edward laments for his wasted songs.

[19] Sonnets 107-116: The Quarrel.
Wriothesley is freed, but after meeting Edward he tells him he is mad at him (for making the deal?).

Joshua Gray

108.
Is there anything new to say? No,
but my songs are daily prayers.
Eternal lines care nil of time.
Time & Nature are now universal.

109.[20]
Why do you say I wronged you?
You are my soul; I thank James
you are free. You are not nothing now.
I ask for nothing, but for you.

110.
It's true, I have whored my life,
hid truth like a lie -- but to save you.
Truth, bow to James.
Won't you keep a blameless heart?

111.
Elizabeth forced my hand against yours!
My acts will be misunderstood
given time. I am not bitter.
Pity me. Have some compassion.

112.
My disgrace is nothing if you let it be.
Disgraced or no, you're my judge.
Profound abyss, take my cares.
You are my one and all.

---

[20] 109: There seems to be an argument between Wriothesley and Edward after 108 was written; Wriothesley is critical of his father.

The Life and Death of King Edward

113.[21]
Since seeing you, I see you
in my mind. My eyes see only
what it will, but shapes sight as you.
My mind turns all images to lies.

114.
Is my mind drunk with flattery?
Does alchemy turn disgrace to harmony?
My mind drinks, not my eye.
If poisoned, only my eye is ill.

115.
Songs that said I could've loved you more
lied. The Queen's to blame for blood's curse.
I called you King despite my fear.
You are blood.

116.
Look, divine right is unchanged
in the changing crown. It is ever-fixed.
The line bears life eternal.
If I'm wrong, I am no poet.

---

[21] 113: Wriothesley and Edward have met face-to-face.

Joshua Gray

THE OBLATION (117-126)
April 20 – 29, 1603

> In this concluding chapter of the 100-sonnet center, Edward continues to defy Time itself – that is, the official record of history. "Thy registers and thee I both defy," he roars, adding, "For thy records and what we see doth lie." (124) He marks the Queen's funeral on April 28, 1603 by offering his "oblation" or sacrifice to Henry while also banishing Time, the "suborned informer" (125) who will testify falsely. This monument contains the truth of Henry's life and blood, however, and therefore nature's final "audit" or accounting of him (126) will eventually be rendered.

117.
Accuse me of neglect,
say I've dined with fools, & sailed far away;
list faults, take aim but do not kill.
I only wanted to help.

118.
We've taken bitter pills; for you
I've fed on bitter food, for health.
Your one day became my life.
I poisoned me to save you.

119.
Such foul tears wet mirrored tales.
Such errors for blessed hearts.
Goodness made best with evil.
I gain you by killing another me.

120.
My No-Son, I've not steel-strength.
Were you wronged by my guilty verdict?
I was wounded by your day.
I ransomed you, you must ransom me.

The Life and Death of King Edward

121.[22]
It's better to be base than thought
so but not. Weak spies make
commoners royal! I am that I am.
Stone-throwers show their own sin.

122.
My songs are memorized. Take them.
They are forever in history.
I give them to you, put them in your trust.
I no longer want them.

123.
Time, I change not; all else does.
Death is near. People think
what they will. I defy you & your history.
I will tell my own truth.

124.
Is my son just a fatherless bastard?
No. He was a planned child!
He schemes, yet is very wise.
Come all & hear the royal truth.

---

[22]"Oxford's haughty declaration of identity, 'I am that I am', which is also a declaration of royalty, echoes God's words to Moses...and is to my knowledge to be found in only one other place in the secular literature of Elizabethan England, and that is in Shakespeare's sonnet 121."-- Charles Beauclerk, *Shakespeare's Lost Kingdom*

125.[23]
Do I care I didn't carry the canopy?
I have seen courting men lose all.
I dishonor her alone, suborned, torn
by Time, the false informer.

126.
My son, you hold the hourglass.
As you freely grow, Nature plucks you
from Death's grasp, but know not forever.
(Farewell, my son.)

---

[23] 125 was written the day of Elizabeth's funeral and is the penultimate sonnet of this dynastic diary.

The Life and Death of King Edward

THE SECOND 26
Edward to Elizabeth

"TWO LOVES I HAVE"
THE DARK LADY (127-152)
February 8, 1601 – March 24, 1603

This sequence consists of twenty-six sonnets in order to balance the first sequence of twenty-six written to Henry, thereby creating a perfect and elegant 26-100-26 design.

Edward writes to Elizabeth during the time of their son's imprisonment up to her death and the succession of James. He accuses her of harboring "a bastard shame" (127) because of their unacknowledged son and her refusal, even while he's a prisoner, to name him in succession. (She will not name anyone!) He does acknowledge that she spared Henry from execution ("Straight in her heart did mercy come" – 145); but otherwise she has driven him to the brink of madness (147) over having lied for her, over and over, thereby keeping secret the fact of Henry's royal blood. His final words to Elizabeth Tudor (152) consist of an accusation that she has forced him to perjure himself, out of loyalty to her, and she has made him "swear against the truth so foul a lie."

This "monument" of sonnets becomes a kind of message in a bottle, set adrift on the sea of Time, carrying the Truth and hopefully reaching the far distant shores of readers in the future.

127.[24]
Our bastard is your disgraced heir.
Royal blood's a nameless disgrace.
You are black as Death, mourning
your son, disgraced by you.

---

[24]Sonnets 127-152, the Dark Lady series, chronologically aligns with 27-105 and begins the night of the rebellion. The series is addressed to Elizabeth instead of Wriothesley. All mentions of "dark" and "black" are metaphorical.

128.
As you play your notes, me beside you,
I envy the chords. Would you exchange
your blood for music's lips?
Give me your voice.

129.
Your cruel treason of demise
is designed to make us insane.
You've beheaded his royalty.
Praise the Queen, but not the mother.

130.
You've red eyes, loose boobs & wig-hair.
Your breath wilts roses.
You're no goddess, but a female slug.
Yet, you made a royal son.

131.
You are no better than your father!
You have the power to kill him;
yet if you do, you will mourn,
and be disgraced yourself.

132.
I serve you, even if you disgrace me,
Our son is not as royal as the sky.
Let your sadness pity me. Have mercy
& you'll have glory.

133.
Your heart wounds me and him.
You treat him ill and deprive all three.
Replace your heart with mine;
send me to your prison too.

The Life and Death of King Edward

134.
I'll lose my name to save your son!
You want glory, but he's our son!
You loan your line, sue defaulters!
Lose him, lose me too.

135.[25]
The royal will, my name Will: yours.
Another's will is royal. Mine isn't.
A rich will adds will still.
Save your son, & your Will.

136.
Admit I was your Will, fulfill your blood!
This Will fills your will with royalty!
I am nothing; he is something.
My name is Will!

137.
The blind lady blinds me. Blindness
takes her will from him!
My heart's in the Tower; my eyes aren't.
False hope is itself false.

138.
You lie! I am not stupid. I am
neither naive nor young. Admit falsehood.
Yet, I should not trust you.
We lie to each other.

---

[25] 135: Why would a poet whose name is Will insist on shouting his name in his poem? The traditional reading doesn't make sense.

139.
(My son and I are one.) Unkind woman,
do not wound me or slay me.
Powerful foe, fight off powerful foes.
Kill me. End my sorrow.

140.
Don't strain my silence or I'll speak out!
If you hate, tell white lies or
I might grow mad and speak ill
of you. Look to the pain.

141.
My heart loves what my eyes despise.
None of my senses want you,
but with wit, they still serve you.
Delusion is my friend.

142.
You hate my royal sin. It warrants
no reproof from you, with your crimes.
Pity him, and be pitied.
Kill him & you have no heir.

143.
Like a neglectful mother eyeing another,
her child cries for attention,
so you run to no one while he wants a mother.
Have some balls.

144.
He is lovely; you are evil.
You tempt him away from me.
Does he revolt within hell's prison?
I fear still, until he's King.

The Life and Death of King Edward

145.
You hated him, but saw my sorrow
and mercifully freed him!
Royal joy follows royal sadness!
You saved his life; you saved me!

146.[26]
You disgrace England & waste your line.
Will worms devour your heir?
Live on me & waste your son.
Feed on Death that feeds on him.

147.
Love is a fever; reason is a doctor.
(Forget my bargain; let truth be told.)
I've gone incurably mad.
You've gone black as hell.

148.
Love gave me false eyes.
I see royal, or common presents well.
Teary eyes restrict my clear sight.
Cunning blood, I see your truth.

149.
I am your servant to the cruelest end.
Your enemies are also mine.
I do as you command. Dark lady,
destroy him and I will approve.

---

[26] 145: Wriothesley is spared but given life imprisonment.
146: Edward protests.

Joshua Gray

150.
You rule and call my truth a liar.
When did blood become horrific?
You taught me to love you more!
If error raised me, I am worthy.

151.
Royal liar, do not urge me against blood.
Betrayer, my body betrays my soul.
I stand and bow for you,
rise and fall for your blood.

152.
You broke your bed-vow of an heir.
You broke two oaths; I lied much more.
I said you were a goddess.
I lie to myself by lying with you.

The Life and Death of King Edward

EPILOGUE
Edward

154.
Our just-born still-bore
His royal might as virgins danced about.
You tried to hide your own blood
But I breathed his coals to fire.

Joshua Gray

The Life and Death of King Edward

Epitaph

The Phoenix and Turtle

Background Notes

If there is any one thing more enigmatic than Shakespeares Sonnets, it's his The Phoenix and Turtle, *published in 1601 in the months after the Essex Rebellion. The orthodox view, as expressed in* The Riverside Shakespeare *(1975) aptly sums up the problem:*

"Shakespeare's poem *The Phoenix arid Turtle* is unique among his works--there is nothing else like it. ... The poem is in three sections. The first five stanzas call up a funeral procession of birds to mourn; the next eight stanzas arc an anthem, presumably sung by the mourners, in which Reason is confounded by Love as exemplified in the phoenix and the turtle. The final section, in a different verse form, is a *threnos;* or *threne* — a lament for the dead---composed by Reason. ... Looking for references to things outside the poem is probably less profitable than to pay attention to the way the poem works. ... The poem moves into the abstract so far that an abstraction within the poem, Reason, cries out and composes a song which solemnly declares the burial of the abstractions Truth and Beauty and returns to the specific and concrete:"

The Oxfordian view, of course, does look for "things outside the poem" in order to understand it. In 1586 Oxfordian William Plumer Fowler wrote: "This poem ... is Oxford's reaction to the Essex Rebellion, the final and greatest tragedy of his life." In this Oxfordian view, the Turtledove is the Poet of the Sonnets (Oxford, Truth), and the Phoenix is the Dark Lady (Elizabeth, Beauty).

"If you saw what I see when I close my eyes, you would not ask me to do it." — Queen Elizabeth, days before she died.

Figure 10 - Queen Elizabeth, The Phoenix Portrait

"It's a funeral dirge in very sparse language, a great artist rising to the maximum of his maturity and honing it down to the bare bones. "Truth and beauty buried be ... For these dead bird's sigh a prayer." — Hank Whittemore

"Shakespeare didn't write a formal elegy to Queen Elizabeth when she died and, of course, had he been William Shaksper of Stratford, he most definitely would. I mean he was in effect the poet laureate. It would be expected of him, and his silence would be construed in a very negative way, but, of course, if Shakespeare was Oxford, then how could he ... I think that Oxford gave his tribute to Elizabeth ... through *The Phoenix and the Turtle* ... that mysterious elegiac poem." — Charles Beauclerk

> [Both quotes above come from the 2011 documentary film *Last Will. & Testament*].

On the following page is the third section of the poem, the *Threnos* ("lament for the dead"), which is as eloquent a summation of the Elizabethan era as any ever published. When Truth is seen as Oxford and Beauty as Elizabeth, it makes perfect, tragic sense.

The Life and Death of King Edward

THRENOS
Phoenix and Turtle

Beauty, Truth, and Rarity,
Grace in all simplicity,
Here enclos'd, in cinders lie.

Death is now the phoenix' nest,
And the turtle's loyal breast
To eternity doth rest;

Leaving no posterity:
'Twas not their infirmity,
It was married chastity.

Truth may seem but cannot be;
Beauty brag but 'tis not she;
Truth and beauty buried be.

To this urn let those repair
That are either true or fair;
For these dead birds sigh a prayer.

Figure 11 - Queen Elizabeth's Funeral Procession

Joshua Gray

The Life and Death of King Edward

BIBLIOGRAPHY/SUGGESTED READING

THE SONNETS - EDITIONS

Beeching, H. C., *The Sonnets of Shakespeare,* 1904
Booth, Stephen, *Shakespeare's Sonnets,* 1977-2000
Dowden, Edward, *The Sonnets of William Shakespeare,* 1881
Duncan-Jones, Katherine, *Arden Shakespeare's Sonnets,* 1997
Evans, G. Blakemore, *The Sonnets,* 1996
Ingram, W. S., & Redpath, Theodore, *Shakespeare's Sonnets,* 1965
Kerrigan, John, *The Sonnets and A Lover's Complaint,* 1986/1999
Rowse, A. L., *Shakespeare's Sonnets: The Problems Solved,* 1st edition, 1964
Rowse, A. L., *Shakespeare's Sonnets: The Problems Solved,* 2nd edition, 1973
Tucker, T G., *The Sonnets of Shakespeare,* 1924
Whittemore, Hank, *The Monument,* 2005*
Wilson, Dover, *The New Shakespeare: The Sonnets,* 1966
Wright, Louis, *Shakespeare's Sonnets* (Folger), 1967

THE SONNETS – COMMENTARY

Acheson, Arthur, *Mistress Davenant• The Dark Lady of Shakespeare's Sonnets,* 1913
Auden, W. H., *Introduction to Signet Classic, The Sonnets,* 1964

Baldwin, T. W., *On the Literary Genetics of Shakespeare's Poems & Sonnets,* 1950

Dodd, Alfred, *The Mystery of Shake-Speare's Sonnets,* 1947

Fort, J. A., *A Time Scheme for Shakespeare's Sonnets,* 1929

Fowler, Alastair, *Triumphal Forms,* 1970

Frye, Northrop, *The Riddle of Shakespeare's Sonnets,*

Giroux, Robert, *The Book Known as Q,* 1982

Greenwood, Sir George, *The Shakespeare Problem Restated,* 1908**

Hotson, Leslie, *Mr. W H,* 1964

Hubler, Edward, *The Sense of Shakespeare's Sonnets,* 1952

Knight, G. Wilson, *The Mutual Flame,* 1962

Knight, G. Wilson, *The Sovereign Flower,* 1958

Lewis, C. S., *English Literature in the Sixteenth Century,* 1954

Malone, Edmund, *Supplement* (to edition of 1778), 1780 Massey, Gerald, *The Secret Drama of Shakespeare's Sonnets Unfolded,* 1866-72

Mathew, Frank, *An Image of Shakespeare,* 1922

Pequigney, Joseph, *Such is My Love: A Study of Shakespeare's Sonnets,* 1985

Rendall, Gerald H., *Personal Clues in Shakespeare Poems & Sonnets,* 1934

Robertson, J.M., *The Problems of the Shakespeare Sonnets,* 1926

Rollins, Hyder Edward, *A New Variorum Edition of Shakespeare: The Sonnets, vol. 2,* 1944

Rush, Peter. *Hidden in Plain Sight,* 2015*

Vendler, Helen, *The Art of Shakespeare's Sonnets,* 1997

Wait, R. J. C., *The Background to Shakespeare's Sonnets,* 1972

The Life and Death of King Edward

Wilson, Dover, *Shakespeare's Sonnets, An Introduction for Historians and Others,* 1963
Wyndham, George, *The Poems of Shakespeare,* 1898

ELIZABETH I

Camden, William, *Annales,* 1615 & 1625; hypertext edition, Dana F. Sutton
Chamberlain, Frederick, *The Private Character of Queen Elizabeth,* 1920
Cole, Mary Hill, *The Portable Queen: Elizabeth I and the Politics of Ceremony,* 1999
Erickson, Carrolly, *The First Elizabeth,* 1983
Guy, John, ed., *The Reign of Elizabeth I: Court and Culture in the Last Decade,* 1995
Haigh, Christopher, *Elizabeth I. Profiles in Power,* 1988; 1998
Jenkins, Elizabeth, *Elizabeth and Leicester,* 1961
Levin, Carole, *The Heart and Stomach of a King,* 1994
Nichols, John, *Progresses and Public Processions of Queen Elizabeth,* 1823
Shell, Marc, *Elizabeth's Glass,* 1993
Sitwell, Edith, *The Queens and the Hive,* 1962
Strickland, Agnes, *Elizabeth,* 1906
Strong, Roy, *The Cult of Elizabeth,* 1977
Strong, Roy, *Elizabeth R,* 1971
Weir, Alison, *The Life of Elizabeth I,* 1998
Williams, Neville, *The Life and Times of Elizabeth I,* 1972

Joshua Gray

PRINCESS ELIZABETH AND THOMAS SEYMOUR (1548-1549)

Cutting, Bonner Miller. "She will not be a mother."*Brief Chronicles*. (III, Fall 2011, pp. 169-199)
Erickson, Caroly, *The First Elizabeth*, 1983 (pp. 65-79)
Hibbert, Christopher, *The Virgin Queen*, 1992 (p. 29)
Skidmore, Chris, *Edward VI: Lost King of England*, 2007 (pages 71-87)
Streitz, Paul, *Oxford, Son of Elizabeth*, 2001
Weir, Alison, *The Life of Elizabeth I*, 1998 (pp. 14-15)

THE EARL OF SOUTHAMPTON

Akrigg, G. P. V., *Shakespeare and the Earl of Southampton*, 1968
Drake, Nathan, *Shakespeare and His Times*, 1817
Green, Martin, *Wriothesley's Roses*, 1993
Rollet, John. "Was Southampton Regarded as the Son of the Queen?" (*De Vere Society newsletter*, July 2000, pp. 19-26)
Rowse, A. L., *Shakespeare's Southampton*, 1965
Stopes, Charlotte Carmichael, *The Life of Henry, Third Earl of Southampton*, 1922

OXFORD'S LETTERS & POEMS

Chiljan, Katherine, *Letters and Poems of Edward Earl of Oxford*, 1998
Fowler, William Plumer, *Shakespeare Revealed in Oxford's Letters*, 1986
May, Steven W., *The Elizabethan Courtier Poets*, 1999
May, Steven W., *The Poems of Edward de Vere, Seventeenth Earl of Oxford and of Robert Devereux,*

The Life and Death of King Edward

Second Earl of Essex (Studies in Philology), Early Winter, 1980

OXFORD AS SHAKESPEARE – AUTHORSHIP BOOKS

Allen, Percy, *The Case for Edward de Vere, 17th Earl of Oxford, as "Shakespeare,"* 1930
Allen, Percy, *The Life Story of Edward de Vere as "William Shakespeare"*, 1932
Anderson, Mark, *Shakespeare By Another Name,* 2005
Beauclerk, Charles, *Shakespeare's Lost Kingdom,* 2010
Caruana, Stephanie & Sears, Elizabeth, *Oxford's Revenge,* 1989
Clark, Eva Turner, *Hidden Allusions in Shakespeare's Plays,* 1931; Miller ed., 1974
Dickinson, Warren, *The Wonderful Shakespeare Mystery,* 2002
Ford, Gertrude, *A Rose By Any Name,* 1964
Hess, Ron, *The Dark Side of Shakespeare, vols. 1-4,* 2002+
Holmes, Edward, *Discovering Shakespeare,* 2001
Looney, J. T., *"Shakespeare" Identified,* 1920
Miller, Ruth Loyd, *"Shakespeare Identified" and Oxfordian Vistas,* 1975
Nelson, Alan, *Monstrous Adversary,* 2003
Ogburn, Dorothy and Charlton, *The Renaissance Man of England,* 1947
Ogburn, Dorothy and Charlton, *This Star of England,* 1950
Ogburn Jr., Charlton, *The Mysterious William Shakespeare,* 1984, 1992
Ogburn, Jr., Charlton, *The Man Who Was Shakespeare,* 1995
Sears, Elisabeth, *Shakespeare and the Tudor Rose,* 1991; Meadow Geese, 2002

Sobran, Joseph, *Alias Shakespeare*, 1997
Streitz, Paul, *Oxford, Son of Queen Elizabeth I*, 2001
Stritmatter, Roger A., *Edward de Vere's Geneva Bible*, 2001
Ward, B.M., *The Seventeenth Earl of Oxford*, 1928
Whalen, Richard E., *Shakespeare: Who Was He? The Oxford Challenge*, 1994
Whittemore, Hank, *100 Reasons Shake-speare was Oxford*, 2016.

OXFORD AS SHAKESPEARE – FILMS

Anonymous (2011, Sony Entertainment)
Shakespeare Mystery, The (1989, documentary, PBS)
Last Will. & Testament (2011, documentary)

OXFORD AS SHAKESPEARE (WEBSITES AND BLOGS)

Hank Whittemore's Shakespeare Blog (hankwhittemore.wordpress.com)

De Vere Society (www.deveresociety.co.uk/)

Edevere17.com (edevere17.com)

Six Degrees of Shakespeare (sixdegreesofshakespeare.wordpress.com)

Shakespeare's Bible (shakespeares-bible.com)

Shakespeare Oxford Fellowship (www.shakespeareoxfordfellowship.org)

The Life and Death of King Edward

ABOUT THE AUTHOR

When Joshua Gray was a teenager, he went to the mountains of Hiawassee, Georgia, with his family to visit his grandparents. There, in their carpeted finished basement, he saw his father reading a big fat book called *The Mysterious William Shakespeare*.

Gray's first distrust of the status quo belief in the man from Stratford came in college, when he questioned Shakespeare's frequent method of non-communication; in other words, why doesn't Claudio confront Hero before the wedding and discover that his eyes had deceived him? Armed with an unconvincing argument by a professor, his answer came full circle when he asked his father, and discovered Edward de Vere.

www.ingramcontent.com/pod-product-compliance
Lightning Source LLC
Chambersburg PA
CBHW071706040426
42446CB00011B/1932